Equipping
Fathers
to Lead
in Family Worship

By

Kenneth S. Coley, Ed.D. &

Blair D. Robinson, D.Min.

randall house

Dedication

Ken: To my grandsons—Coley, Haddon, and Rowan. May they continue to grow in their worship of Jesus.

Blair: To my Dad, who faithfully taught me about the glory of God; To my wife, Lauren, who I am blessed to teach the glory of God with; To my children, Abel, Titus, and Abi-Ruth, who with joy I teach the glory of God to.

Table of Contents

Introduction to

Equipping Fathers to Lead in Family Worship

By Dr. Ken Coley

Many Saturdays when I was a young father, my son and I spent the morning at our church gym with a gang of friends who played together, while Scott played with the sons of my buddies. While we moved back and forth in full-court games, the five-year-olds would relentlessly dribble miniature balls up and down the sidelines mimicking our movements. After a couple of hours of vigorous play, we would head home for a shower and lunch.

But something unexpected happened on this particular winter afternoon. I was in the basement of our three-story townhouse when I heard an unusual thumping sound echoing in the stairwell. It continued from the top floor to the first floor, getting louder as it approached. I hurried to check on the noisy commotion when I came face to face with my son on the stairs. Scott had put on my sweaty socks and pulled them up to his hips and had knotted my high-top basketball shoes so they would stay on his tiny feet. I was amazed he took care to dress in my outfit from the morning, still damp from perspiration, and even more surprised he had not fallen down the stairs in the clumsy, oversized shoes.

For a few brief moments, I stood stunned like few other times in my adult life. In an instant, I discovered a truth that would change my life:

Your son is going to be just like you.

Have you identified this in the children the Lord has called you to lead? I imagine you have, but have you reflected on the long-lasting,

1

even eternal significance of this truth? Maybe your son will decide to dress like you, with his baseball cap or work gloves that match yours. Or maybe he will follow you around the backyard wanting to cut grass with you. My daughter was not to be denied and grew up playing soccer, baseball, and basketball with me and her older brother. And we all read together every night, and they both became English majors in college, just like their dad. But there are far more important things for dads to consider.

What will you teach your sons and daughters to worship?

Our American culture has its own powerful attractions, but when you really think about it, so have all cultures throughout history. The Lord warned Moses about the wayward hearts of His children: "Then take care lest you forget the LORD, who brought you out of the land of Egypt, out of the house of slavery" (Deuteronomy 6:12). When MTV first began in the early 1980s, I recall hearing someone say, "The network doesn't plan to just influence them; they want to own them." Certainly, that was just one of a multitude of media influences that would have an ever-increasing hold on successive generations. Something closer to home than MTV, however, bumped the mesmerizing media from our children's radar.

During our kids' most formative years their mom drove them to school. These trips included everyone in the car listening to a diverse collection of whatever my wife was teaching the choir that week: famous hymns, inspiring black gospel, quartets with tight harmonies, and contemporary Christian melodies with guitars and drums. They heard it all, and often sang along. Many of those tunes and lyrics remain in their active memories today.

But tragically, many people have not heeded the words of the Lord given to Moses during his leadership in the Sinai Desert: (as recorded in Deuteronomy 6:5, 7) you should love the Lord your God with all your heart and with all of your soul and with all of your strength.

And teach them to your children.

This book is, primarily, a guide for pastors to equip fathers to lead family worship in their homes but can ultimately serve all fathers as well. Children are designed to observe and follow their parents as we model what it means to worship the one true God. They are eternally designed to observe us and follow our lead as we model what it means to worship the one true God. But we realize that teaching your children to say a blessing before the family mealtime and a prayer before bed might be all you are prepared to do. Can we agree that family worship needs to be so much more?

As authors, parents, and fellow sojourners, we are eager to present biblical concepts about the basics of family worship so you can look forward to modeling for your congregation and your family a joyful celebration of our relationship with our Heavenly Father. We want to encourage you to *impress them (the commandments) on their hearts* by sharing meaningful daily worship. This starts with asking the Holy Spirit to transform you, the parent and leader of your home.

The Example of Ezra

One of the lesser-known teachers and leaders of the nation of Israel was Ezra, who was chosen by God to lead the second wave of Israelites out of exile and back to Jerusalem. Repeatedly in the book that is named after him, we read that *the hand of the Lord his God was upon him* (Ezra 7:6, 28; 8:18, 22, 31). Early on in the background information about this faithful leader, we get a glimpse into his life and learn what set him apart: "For Ezra had set his heart to study the Law of the Lord, and to do it and to teach his statutes and rules in Israel" (7:10). Take note of the sequence: first came study, then observance, followed by teaching. May we be men like this!

Ezra's monumental contributions are overshadowed by Nehemiah, the leader of the third wave of returnees. But it should be noted that on the momentous day of celebration following the completion of the re-building of the wall around Jerusalem, Nehemiah tapped Ezra to stand with him and *lead worship* (Nehemiah 8).

Looking for the "Ancient Paths"

In a post-pandemic world that has changed how society interacts and with a culture that is ever shifting and attempting to redefine God's design for households, may this book serve as a fresh encouragement to return to the "ancient paths" where Jeremiah says is the good way for God's people to walk (Jeremiah 6:16). The ancient paths refer to God's Word and the ways He has designed His people to live in obe-dient fellowship with Him. Truly, there is no new thing under the sun (Ecclesiastes 1:9).

So, we begin with an overview of biblical and historical thinking about worship in general and family worship in particular so fathers can be convinced of God's design for the home and equipped to lead. Next, we challenge you to strengthen your relationship with the Lord as you grow personally as a faithful follower and worshiper. These two steps are vital as you prepare to then show the way with your family and coach others in your ministry.

This work also presents some creative ways to go about leading your tribe as you walk the ancient paths. It might be of interest to you to know that this undertaking is applauded by the latest mind, brain, and education research, and we'll be weaving some of these instruction-al ideas into the chapters on planning your daily worship time. Siegel and Bryson point out to parents that as they use everyday moments as points of connection and instruction, parents can significantly impact their children's cognitive and emotional growth toward integration.[1]

As Leaders, We Should ...

Know the Ancient Paths ... Walk the Ancient Paths ...
and Point to the Ancient Paths

Have we convinced you it's time for you to lead? Referring back to an earlier discussion, we want to do our part to prepare you to be an Ezra in your home and church. We want to encourage you toward this important role in three ways:

Know the ancient paths. In **chapters 1-3** you will strengthen your understanding of God's plan for you to lead worship in your home as you examine the biblical and historical perspectives of this important dimension of family life. In addition, you will get a biblical overview of what the elements of reading, praying, and singing look like on an everyday basis.

Walk the ancient paths. In **chapters 4-7** you will transition to modeling for your children what growing in your faith looks like in your life. We want to equip you to grow personally to lead in prayer, in worship, and in teaching.

Point to the ancient paths. In **chapters 8-9** you will be challenged to model this approach to family worship with other fathers in your church. We have accepted the challenge to develop training resources so you and other fathers can grow together as you raise up a generation of men in your community, just as Ezra was for his Israelite caravan returning from exile.

May it be said of you as you lead your family and your community of believers ...

The hand of the Lord was upon him.

Endnotes

[1] Siegel and Bryson, *The Whole-Brain Child Approach* (New York, NY: Bantam Books, 2012), 10.

PART 1

KNOW THE
ANCIENT PATHS

CHAPTER 1

The Biblical Mandate for Family Worship

This chapter will attempt to provide an explanation from God's Word of how God designed the home to function. God has provided the heads of households to lead their families in instruction and in the praise of His name. To build the argument, this chapter will look more closely at Deuteronomy 6:4-9 and Ephesians 6:1-4. Beginning the work by examining God's Word lays a convictional foundation for the rest of the book.

In God's care for His people, He has intentionally and strategically designed the home as a place of worship. Specifically, a place for His people to worship Him—the one and only God of the universe. His design comes with great provision. Most generously, God provides Himself as the primary caretaker and overseer of His households, providing His Word with covenants and promises attached. God provides a way of fellowship through His Son, Jesus, who is the Creator, atoning sacrifice, Redeemer, Resurrection, and King for His people. He provides His Spirit who convicts, guides, and produces fruit in His people for His glory. He is our great provision. He is our great gift. He is the good news.

God has also designed the home to be led by men who love Him with full hearts and who fear Him. He has instructed these men to faithfully fulfill the responsibilities to lead, serve, and shepherd those in their homes (Ephesians 6:4). These are men who yield to Christ as the head of their families, and who lead their families toward Him no matter the cost; men who trust His Word, teach His Word, rejoice in His Word, and pray according to His Word. Yes, this is God's good design for the home.

This examination and request for men to lead their home is certainly not to suggest that women do not play an essential role in the home as well because they absolutely do. They too are a significant piece of God's provision for the household. They teach children and serve as a model of faithfulness for them to observe (Proverbs 1:8; 31:28). They too are called to love God with their heart, soul, and might (Deuteronomy 6:5), and they are called to promote their husband's leadership and keep him accountable to leading his household (Genesis 2:18; Ephesians 5:22). Women are to be cherished in the home the same way that Christ cherishes His bride, the Church. There are times when women must take the lead role in leading the family to worship God, such as when the father is unavailable or unconverted. In God's provision, we see that Timothy's mother and grandmother were responsible for training him in the faith early in his life, with no mention of his father in the Scriptures (2 Timothy 1:5; 3:14-15). However, this particular book will focus on the father's role and responsibility in caring for and leading the home, as is described in Scripture.

If you are a pastor, this is what God has laid out for His people, and we have a specific responsibility to shepherd and equip His people for such a task as those who will give an account of their souls (Hebrews 13:17). A faithful brother once asked me, "What has God required of you as a pastor?" I responded with examples such as, "Shepherd His people, faithfully teach the Scriptures, provide Gospel-centered counseling, lead by example, etc." His response I will not forget, "God expects the same for a father in his home." To build the argument for God's design, we must first be convinced (and convicted) by what God's Word says on the matter of family worship and the role of father. The Scripture speaks directly to the matters of the home and the blessing of passing along the Word of God and works of God to the next generation. Though there is simply not enough time to exegete all biblical passages that relate to this topic, looking intently at two texts should be enough to begin a conviction.

A framework before we dive in:

Fathers, we do not have the capabilities or power to move our children spiritually. It is the grace and kindness of God that grows your children spiritually through the work of the Holy Spirit. The work and glory belong to Him. Yet, we do not stand idly by, for God has given us responsibilities to cultivate, encourage, pray, and instruct them. Our children are to know they are loved ... even if they do not love the Lord you love. Guard yourself with this truth as we begin, as it will help you depend upon the God of all wisdom and power.

Deuteronomy 6:4-9

After roaming the wilderness for forty years, Israel stood at the precipice of their Promised Land and received from God through Moses the Book of Deuteronomy. Deuteronomy is instruction centered on ensuring Israel's faithful devotion to God as His covenant people when entering Canaan. Deuteronomy provides an extensive educational plan for God's people in which it was intended that every person in the nation, and future generations, would be trained from (cf. Deuteronomy 4:9, 10; 6:7, 20; 11:19; 31:13; 32:7, 46). Deuteronomy 4, 5, and 6, emphasize the charge of God's words to the coming generations specifically, most notably emphasized in Deuteronomy 6:6-9. Moses calls the Israelites to focus on their children and their children's children. Due to God's exclusive preservation and covenant for His people, He expected Israel to be faithful in following Him, worshiping Him, and training up generation after generation who hold to the same faith and obedience to God as the generation of Israel who received this instruction first.

Preserving the nation through the training of the next generation is a critical subject in the book of Deuteronomy, and the responsibility lands with Israel to do so. With this responsibility, God's people are concurrently urged not to forget who God is, what He has done for them, or that they are accountable to pass along the truths and history of God to their children. Forgetting to do this opens the whole nation up to the great risk that their children will not know or worship the God of salvation. Israel was commanded to remember, and guard against forgetting, what God had asked of them when entering the land.

The *Shema*

Though this command is apparent throughout Deuteronomy, chapter 6:4-9 highlights this command and warning. Jewish tradition terms this passage as the *Shema*, which means "to hear," named after the first word of verse 4. The *Shema* delivers the Lord's instruction to Israel to teach the future generations, setting up what would become the core of daily Jewish worship. "Hear, O Israel," in verse 4, or "listen up" Israel, as we would understand today, is a directive to pay attention and consider the attributes of God and to heed the following teaching. And God can command this, because He is the one, unique, undivided God in all of creation. When He speaks, His people are called to listen, worship, and obey.

The *Shema* then moves from who God is to what the people of Israel are called to do. Verse 5 says "You shall love," as Israel receives an invitation to respond in love to God "with all your heart and with all your soul and with all your might." Summarizing this phrase in a helpful way, J. W. Turner and Ken Coley use their expertise to suggest that after Moses reviewed the Ten Commandments in Deuteronomy 5, he declared in the *Shema*, "Obey the Lord your God exclusively with all your innermost personal reflections; with all your outermost public expressions; and with all your efforts and exertions."[1] The idea stressed giving one's entire self to God and His commands. In essence, this type of devotion to God creates a deep culture of committed worship.

Despite Deuteronomy's attention to obedience from the immediate audience of Israel, the secondary element of the passage focuses on educating the coming generations of Israel, as already discussed. When individuals love God, they are to teach the next generation to do the same thing. This instruction was to be purposeful, regular, and routine (Deuteronomy 4:9 and 6:2). Fundamentally, verses 6-9 convey to Israel how they can remain mindful of God, as family worship becomes an essential theme for the people of God to carry out their own worship and also the worship of their lineage.

For this little book, the focus is on God's instruction in verse 7. Verse 7 says, "You shall teach them diligently to your children," which represents the transmitting of "these words" from parents to their children. Parents must first internalize and then pass these commands from God to the next generation. The word *teach* in this passage refers to more than mere speaking. Turner and Coley emphasize that the word "teach" in Hebrew pedagogy, "cannot be separated from the qualifier before it in verse 6: 'These words that I command you today shall be on your heart,'" and thus families should practice them so consistently in effort to pierce the conscience and mindfulness of the children in the home.[2] Our teaching becomes the "impressing" of *these words*. It's how we fix the truth deeply in one's mind. The Hebrew word for *teach* in verse 7 is the word *sh-n-n* (*shinan*), which means *repeat*.[3] In some places of Scripture, this root word (*shinan*) simply means "repeat" (cf. Proverbs 17:9). However, in verse 7, the word suggests a particular kind of repetition— that of a constant sharpening.[4] One scholar provides the imagery of this word in action as that of a stone worker who is methodically hammering and chiseling a slab of granite in effort to create a lasting message.[5] The work is tiring. At times it feels like progress isn't happening. Yet the constant hammering in and inscribing of these words helps to create a lasting message on the children's hearts. Therefore, parents repeat, *blow by blow*, the truth, grace, and glory of God to their children.

The concluding half of verse 7 identifies the specific times parents must discuss *these words* with their children: "and shall talk of them when you sit in your house, and when you walk by the way, and when you lie down, and when you rise." The connotation in the passage suggests that the demands of Yahweh's covenant and the reminders of His faithfulness ought to be the topic of conversation for parents with their children in all settings. Redeeming conversations and specific instruction about God should drive the motives of personal worship and family worship. The responsibility is for these conversations to be the culture of the home—a lifestyle. This passage leaves no room for dichotomies in conversation or in worship. Said another way, God's glory and our need for a Savior should be the *language* of our homes. The Lord and His redemption changes the way we see everything in this world. So, whether we are discussing sports, or relationships, or any other general conversation, God's worth and Word are the bedrock of every conversation.

Ephesians 6:4

Fathers instructing children is not merely an Old Testament concept or a Jewish tradition, however. The Apostle Paul continues this instruction for the Church. In his instruction found in Ephesians 5:22–6:4, Paul focuses exclusively on Christian household relationships and what they should resemble when faithfully carried out. In Ephesians 6:4, Paul focuses on the special responsibilities' fathers have to their children. In considering the context of the passage, with Paul writing to a Greco-Roman culture in Ephesus, he assigns responsibility for the whole family to the fathers, including the education of the children. Paul knew that this reflected the hierarchical structure of the day, as both for Hellenistic-Jews and Greeks and Romans considered fathers the primary leader of the home. However, the demands and harshness in which fathers ruled their homes in these cultures was taught against by Paul.

In verse 4 Paul wrote, "Fathers, do not provoke your children to anger, but bring them up in the discipline and instruction of the Lord." The first part of the verse instructs fathers to not provoke their children, and a similar instruction also occurs in the passage of Colossians 3:21, another which was a similar culture to the Ephesians. Fathers have an obligation in verse 4, not to *provoke* (*parorgizete*) their children ensures that resentment will not be established.[6] Paul introduced a radical new concept within his culture for fathers and a contrasting view from that of the culture of his day. His readers in Ephesus would have culturally promoted the absolute authority of the father. Whatever they said or did was the established rule—and it could not be questioned. For the new culture Paul introduced, considered the feelings of the child and served as a new thought for fathers and households.[7] Fathers not provoking their children, as measured by theologian Andrew Lincoln, would proscribe fathers from such practices as harsh attitudes, words, and actions toward children, excessive and insensitive discipline, abuse of authority, unreasonable rules, subjecting children to humiliation, and overall neglect toward children's needs and feelings.[8] The gospel, which Paul is advocating in this text, redeems all aspects of life, including how a father is to lead his family.

In the second part of verse 4, Paul provided an action plan for Christian fathers. The charge Paul gives, proves simple: "bring them [children] up in the discipline and the instruction of the Lord." This directive from Paul charges fathers to bring up their children in a way that is distinctly Christian and unique to the surrounding culture. To *bring up* (*ektrephete*) implies "to nourish." Fathers are to nurture their children and rear them up from childhood toward maturity and Christlikeness. Paul, then, mentions here two aspects of the educational process for children. Fathers are to raise their children in the "discipline and instruction of the Lord." The word *discipline* (*paideia*) also translates to "training," which in this context, refers to the whole education of a child. This includes the responsibility to discipline, instruct, and foster the child. The second noun, *instruction* (*nouthesia*), translates to "warning" and refers to the verbal educational aspect of bringing up children in the Lord.[9] Both of these are really more similar than different, perhaps even redundant. As verse 4 concludes, fathers are to execute these different forms of training and education assumed "of the Lord." Training and admonition by fathers refer to the Lord's work through fathers as they represent His immediate delegates to His children. The Lord always serves as the reference point in the home for all Christian instruction and discipline by parents when serving as His delegates. Fathers, therefore, instruct, train, admonish, encourage, and discipline their children always with the Lord in mind, serving as His representative to the family.

Think about this, the discipline and instruction given forth by parents as they rear their children … belongs to the Lord. This signifies His great care and love for His people. John Stott believed that not only did the discipline and instruction belong to the Lord, "[but] more than this, namely that behind the parents who teach and discipline their children there stands the Lord himself … as the chief teacher and administrator of discipline."[10] The purpose and hope of this implication is that through the Lord's teaching and instruction children will come to accept the teaching and discipline of the Lord Jesus Christ.[11]

These two passages of Scripture, though offering different aspects of God, His covenant with His people, and paternal responsibility, weave together and proclaim truth passed to each generation from the Old Testament to the New Testament. Deuteronomy 6:4-9 establishes a foundation for the people of God to love Him fully based on *these words* of God given to them through the Mosaic Covenant. His people are to remember *these words* of the commandments, and be careful not to forget them, internalizing the meaning of *these words* and responding in obedience to God. Parents, therefore, have the responsibility to transmit this devotion, allegiance, and love for God with constant repetition in teaching the next generation, which transpires in all settings and conversations. This passage serves as the conceptual bedrock for family worship.

In Ephesians 6, Paul specifically addresses fathers to instruct and discipline their children. Fathers represent the discipline and instruction of the Lord to their children implying that fathers are the regents empowered by God to instruct children toward Him. Therefore, fathers are not only responsible for instruction and discipline, but also serve as God's representatives in the home. Family worship, therefore, as discussed throughout this chapter, provides an opportunity for parents to teach and exemplify *these words*, and the *discipline and instruction of the Lord* to the next generation. Fathers are called to devote themselves to God, diligently teach their children the commands and stories of God, repeat the teaching often, discuss the things of God in every area of life, and understand that they serve their children as representatives of God Himself.

In the next chapter, we will consider the record of family worship chronicled throughout the history of the church. As well, we will analyze the most notable elements that have shaped family worship in the home in hopes of establishing a contingency of helpful practices for the fathers in the local church and the home today.

Endnotes

[1] Ken Coley and John Turner, "Examining Deuteronomy 6 Through the Lens of 21st Century Educational Concepts," *D6FMJ* 3 (2018): 9.

[2] Ibid., 10.

[3] Tigay, Jeffrey H. Deuteronomy: *The Traditional Hebrew Text with the New JPS Translation in the JPS Torah Commentary* (Philadelphia, PA: The Jewish Publication Society, 1996), 78. This differs from the Hebrew word "teach" or *lamad* used in other parts of Deuteronomy (cf. 11:19).

[4] Coley and Turner, "Examining Deuteronomy 6," 10.

[5] Merrill, Eugene, H. *Deuteronomy*. New American Commentary 4 (Nashville, TN: Holman Reference, 1994), 167. Merrill provides a vivid analogy of this work by parents: "The image is that of the engraver of a monument who takes a hammer and chisel in hand and with painstaking care etches a text into the face of a solid slab of granite. The sheer labor of such a task is daunting indeed, but once done the message is there to stay," 167.

[6] Wood, A. Skevington. *Ephesians, Philippians, Colossians, 1, 2 Thessalonians, 1,*

2 Timothy, Titus, Philemon. Expositors Bible Commentary 11 (Grand Rapids, MI: Zondervan, 1978), 82.

[7] Ibid., 81.

[8] Lincoln, Andrew. *Ephesians.* Word Biblical Commentary 42 (Grand Rapids, MI: Zondervan, 1990), 406.

[9] Stott, John R.W. *The Message of Ephesians.* BST 21 (Downers Grove, IL: Inter-Varsity Press, 1979), 248.

[10] Ibid., 249.

[11] Ibid.

Historical Practices of Family Worship in the Church

After reviewing biblical foundations for family worship, chapter 2 will provide a brief primer of family worship throughout the Church's history. This chapter will cover time periods and influencers, practices, and comparisons to today's need to reclaim the role fathers have to serve as "the pastors" in the home. In addition to the history discussed, the chapter will also provide directives and best practices that were used by fathers of the past which can still be relevant for fathers today.

The Historical Practices of Family Worship

Faithful pastors, fathers, and mothers throughout church history have provided a powerful testimony of ministry in the home for us to consider today. Since the resurrection of Christ, the church has encouraged the practice of family worship throughout particular portions and periods in its history. Certainly, not all versions or practices of family worship are healthy in church history, but the church has promoted family worship during certain seasons. Some of the earliest Christians did not neglect the practice of family worship.

The Early Church Practices

Lyman Coleman references that for first generation Christians the family commonly gathered together both in the early morning and again before retiring to bed to read the Scriptures, praise the Lord through song, and pray, thanking the Lord for His provision and protection. Coleman writes of the character traits of the early Christians: "one that stands out more frequently in beautiful and prominent relief … the tender solicitude and the winning arts which they employed to imbue the susceptible minds of the young with the knowledge and faith of the Scripture."[1] The *Didache* refers to such time as mandatory for early Christians by stating to household leaders, "Do not neglect your responsibilities to your children. Begin teaching your children when they are very young to reverently fear God."[2] Ignatius (c. 30–107), Bishop of Antioch, believed Ephesians 6:4 means that Christian fathers should merely teach their children the Bible.[3] The great Polycarp (c. 69–155), in his letter to the Philippians, exhorted fathers and husbands to "[teach] your wives [to walk] in the faith given to them, and in love and purity … and to train their children in the knowledge and fear of God."[4] Tertullian (c.160–225) wrote regarding the faithful practices in the Christian home between husband and wife: "How beautiful, then, the marriage of two Christians, two who are one in hope, one in desire, one in the way of life they follow, one in the religion they practice … They pray together, they worship together, they fast together; instructing one another, encouraging one another, strengthening one another."[5] In describing children's training of the early Christians, Coleman notes, "Thus did the pious care of primitive Christians intermingle religion with all pursuits and recreations of the young … They had been first taught to view everything in the spirit and by the principles of the Word of God."[6] Though not expressly detailed or widely written on, the concept of worship and instruction in the home appears present during the first few centuries of the church, which encouraged specific elements of prayer, praise, and Scripture reading. Additionally, the church challenged fathers and heads of household to fulfill duties to their families as laid forth in the Scripture.

In the fourth century, as recorded by historian Philip Schaff, John Chrysostom (c. 349–407), who served as the archbishop of Constantinople, "urged that every house be a church, and every head of the family a spiritual shepherd, remembering the account he must give even for his children and servants."[7] Schaff also includes Augustine's (c. 354–430) similarly stated comments to his congregation: "It is your duty to put your talent to usury; everyone must be a bishop in his own home; he must see that his wife, his son, his daughter, his servant … continues in the faith."[8] Thus, even into the fourth century, evidence exists of fathers' responsibility for leading worship and study in the home.

Connecting the Early Church to the Reformation

In between the Early Church period and the Reformation, much of the practice of family worship was lost from what we can tell. By the fourth century, the church grew more and more into a top-down form of leadership and structure, with the emphasis more on the clergy and less on the saints and the households. The specific reasons for the diminishment of family worship and the transfer of authority from the household to the clergy are difficult to fully diagnose. However, one reason includes a decrease in men partaking in marriage and family due to the rise of persecution, which led to an increase in celibacy and ultimately monasticism (religiously living isolated from the world). This transference eventually reshaped the ecclesiological focus from the family to the congregation. During this season in the Church, the focus of teaching and knowledge became isolated to the role of bishop and elder, who did not encourage heads of households to fulfill their biblical duties in the home. Bibles were not being used in the home for personal worship or family worship as many families no longer had copies of the Scripture. Worship was limited to attending a worship service or mass. When the Word of God was removed from the people, the people did not flourish, but rather became dependent on the leadership of the congregation.

21

The Reformation: Family Worship and
the Role of Fathers Re-established

One of the central themes of the Reformation was recapturing Scriptural authority (*sola scriptura*) in the church. When the Scripture returned to the hands of individuals in the congregation, family worship began once again to flourish in the home. The great Reformers, Luther and Calvin, both focused on the households and developed a strategy for Christian training and discipleship led by parents in the home.[9] Martin Luther (c. 1483–1546), indelibly impacted the history of family worship. As part of his direct influence on the church during the Reformation, Luther wrote his *Small Catechism* in 1529 and included an appendix on "Household Duties" that was meant to help heads of households to lead their families in Scripture and doctrine study. Luther's catechism introduced the question-and-answer format, which was helpful for memorizing the Scriptures. For Luther, the household was meant to serve as the forum in which God entrusts parents, particularly fathers, with the responsibility to train their children in the Lord.[10] In the preface of his large catechism, Luther wrote, "we must have the young learn parts which belong to the Catechism or instruction for children well and fluently and diligently exercise themselves in them and keep them occupied with them. Therefore, it is the duty of every father of a family to examine his children."[11] Reminiscent of the instruction of the Scripture, and of the theology of other faithful men throughout church history, Luther served a pivotal role in urging fathers to train and examine those in their household.

John Calvin (c.1509–1564), like Luther, also emphasized the importance for fathers to train their children toward godliness, and like Luther, he also produced catechisms to serve as helpful tools for household education.[12] Calvin condensed the principles of his opus, *The Institutes of Christian Religion*, into a catechism for fathers to train their children. In Calvin's comments on Deuteronomy 6:6, he wrote in regard to a father's relationship with his children, "constant conversation should be held about it with their children, in order that fathers should diligently attend and apply themselves to the duty of instruction."[13] Calvin explicitly articulated the theological foundations for discipleship in the home which was a stark contrast to home ministry before the Reformation. Both Calvin and Luther prove helpful in the family-worship conversation as they emphasize the supremacy of the Scriptures for all people and empowered the home, and the fathers of it, to worship the God of the Scriptures.

A reclaiming of household piety occurred throughout the Reformation in countries such as Germany, Switzerland, France, and Holland, but J. W. Alexander writes, "in no country has the light of the dwelling [of family worship] burned more brightly than in Scotland. Family worship, in all its fulness, was coeval with the first Reformation period. Probably no land, in proportion to its inhabitants, ever had so many praying families."[14] John Knox (c. 1514–1572), the man God used to bring about reformation in Scotland, challenged men to lead families in the fear of God, which encouraged an entire nation to reform and consider the Scriptural mandate. Knox authored *The Book of Common Order*, which was the authorized *Book of Worship* in the Church of Scotland for the better part of one-hundred years from 1564–1645. Scotland considered family worship such a necessary duty for fathers that through the Act of Assembly in 1596, it became normal practice for elders to visit homes to catechize fathers and to ensure fathers were leading their families. Ministers asked standard investigatory questions to the heads of families, such as,

- *"Whether God be worshipped in the family by prayers, praises, and reading Scripture?"*
- *"[do members of the household] attend family worship?"*
- *"[Is there] catechizing in the family?"*[15]

If the head of a household failed to fulfill his duty to his family, the elder admonished him privately, and if not repentant, the head of the household would be disciplined by the church. It is crazy for us to think about that happening today! Nevertheless, family worship remained universal throughout Scotland during this time and was practiced both in the large cities and in the rural towns.

The Westminster Confession of Faith and
The Second London Baptist Confession of 1689

In 1643 through 1649, the Westminster Assembly gathered the ancestors of the Reformation from Scotland and England and created an agreed upon statement of faith, the *Westminster Confession of Faith*. Specifically influential in regard to family worship, this document has family ministry in mind. If you read the Westminster Confession, you will note that the preface of the book is geared toward those who lead households; specifically advising them to carry out their responsibilities in the family by knowing the Scriptures themselves and spiritually caring for those under their charge. For the ancestors of the Reformation, putting the Word of God back into the hands of the head of homes, meant the Word of God could flourish in the hearts who hear the Word and receive it.

With the confession completed in 1647, and still carrying forward the concept of family worship, the Church of Scotland issued *The Directory of Family Worship*, which served as a friendly guide for family worship and accompanied the Westminster Confession of Faith as a tool to be used in the home.[16] This directory influenced the Presbyterians throughout Scotland in momentous ways. In August 1647, the General Assembly described the purpose of *The Directory of Family Worship* in this way: "ACT for observing the directions of the General Assembly for secret and private worship, and mutual edification, and censuring such as neglect Family Worship."[17] The General Assembly, carrying forward the previous course from the Act of Assembly in 1596, earnestly recommended to all presbyteries that family worship be set up in every home in their charge. The Presbyterians and Puritans of the day recognized three forms of worship in which God had given authority: congregational worship under the leadership of the Church, private and family worship under the leadership of the head of the household, and individual worship (or personal worship). The General Assembly urged all of Scotland to set up and use these three settings for worship for the sake of "great purity" in the land and in effort to be advanced. *The Directory* charges the head of every household to ensure the practice of both personal worship and family worship in the home.[18] The document also charges the head of the household to urge family members in their own private worship and to lead in prayer and praise, and in the reading of Scripture.[19] These exhortations by the Church of Scotland to fathers in practicing personal worship and then family worship, bring to mind Moses's instruction in Deuteronomy 6:6 to the men of Israel for "these words" to be on their hearts before they diligently teach them to their children in verse 7. Fathers must worship the Lord first before they lead others toward Him, and therefore, teaching men a basic hermeneutic in how to study the Scriptures, and teaching them and encouraging them to be men of prayer, remain important parts of a pastor's responsibility in training the men under his care.

Essential to the practice of family worship is the role of the minister or pastor given charge of the family. Though *The Directory* considered men the heads of their families and responsible for leading worship in the home, it also held ministers accountable for their equipping of men. Written in Section IV of *The Directory*, "the minister is to stir up such as are lazy and train up such as are weak to a fitness for these exercises."[20] This portion of church history ought to help us today, pastors. Consider how serious this responsibility was taken for it to be printed and universally known as the expectation of pastors and ministers. Consider how far we have come from this today, and how little our men are engaging their families with this responsibility. This should encourage us, pastors, to refocus on certain ministry priorities that are good for our people. Pastors, we have a responsibility to keep the Word of God faithfully and accurately before our people. We are to show our people in the text what God has for us there. Through the work of the Spirit in them, our people can be convinced and convicted that what God's Word says is true and good, and therefore must be obeyed. Family worship is essential for a healthy edification of a church congregation, and healthy fathers and heads of households are essential for healthy and thriving family worship. *The Directory of Family Worship* continued the idea that fathers are to represent Christ to their families as the Apostle Paul introduced in Ephesians 6:1-4.

This truth is not so only for Presbyterian brothers, but historically so, for Baptists as well. Like the *Westminster Confession of Faith*, *The Second London Baptist Confession of 1689* states, "but God is to be worshipped everywhere in spirit and in truth; as in private families daily, and in secret each one by himself."[21] Written in the forward to the reader of *The Second Baptist London Confession of 1689* is this charge, "And verily there is one spring and cause of the decay of Religion [sic] in our day, which we cannot but touch upon, and earnestly urge a redress of; and that is the neglect of the worship of God in Families [sic], by those to whom the charge and conduct of them is committed."[22] The charge encourages parents to take responsibility for training and catechizing children during their "tender years" to know the truth of God as revealed in the Scriptures. For Baptists, these family worship convictions survived through the seventeenth century, and were established across the colonization of America.

The Puritans: Family Worship and the Role of Fathers

Also influential in the history and practice of family worship are the Puritans. Puritans were adamant of the practice of family worship in the home for two primary reasons: 1) it was a command and blessing for the households of God's people according to the Word of God, and 2) it was a direct response to the secular assaults experienced by families of the day. The Puritans' robust view of family worship practices and their convictions of the father's role in the home provide helpful guidance for us today as we too significantly experience worldly distractions and temptations. Leland Ryken says, "The age of the Puritans was no stranger to societal assaults on the Christian family. Faced with the same pressures that confront us today, the Puritans formulated a theory of the family that offers some attractive possibilities to our own age."[23] Puritans had such a high view of the institution of the home to worship the Lord because they equated the home with the church. Matthew Henry, a faithful preacher and strong advocate of family worship, wrote, "What that family religion is which will be as a church in the house ... Churches are sacred societies, incorporated for the honor and service of God in Christ; devoted to God, and employed for him; so should our families be."[24] For Puritans, the church is not something that you go to, but the church is something that you are ... and you worshipped as the church personally, in your family, and as a congregation. The emphasis was not placed on buildings, but on gathering. If we are honest, many of the fathers in our congregations might still consider the "church" as a sacred meeting place with certain times and schedules. As pastors, we must encourage fathers to view the church as a *people* and not a *building*.

Puritans wanted to practice God's design throughout every area of their lives, including family worship. They had such a high view of the purpose of the family, and they expected each family member to fulfill his or her God-ordained role.[25] The Puritans based their understanding of headship on Christ's example of loving headship to the church, a headship based on responsibility and driven by love and not authoritarianism.

Horton Davies, the late professor of religious history at Princeton University, in his work called *The Worship of the English Puritans*, further describes the role of fathers in family worship. With family worship as the new expectation from the Reformation given to Puritan families to partake in, Davies underscores promises fathers made at their children's baptisms to oversee their spiritual life, to dutifully train them in the Scriptures, and to lead and instruct them in prayer and in the praise of God.[26] At the very least of their responsibilities, Puritan fathers must catechize their children on the Lord's day [Sundays], but in addition to teaching through the catechism, the church encouraged fathers to lead their families in prayer twice a day.[27] Edmund Morgan, in his book *The Puritan Family*, conveys the importance of the education of children in the Puritan home, primarily reading the Scriptures to know God and His salvation.[28] The conviction to foster knowledge of God's Word copiously throughout their lives, including entrusting the gospel to their children, constituted a response to the Roman [Catholic] Church, whom the Puritans considered to have kept the world in ignorance by hoarding the knowledge of the gospel.[29] As the Catholic Church concealed knowledge of the gospel and the Scriptures, the Puritans responded by educating and training their households, which essentially served as the very antithesis to the Catholic Church.

Puritans ascribed to the doctrine of the "priesthood of all believers," which was developed further from the days of the Reformation. This conviction certainly influenced Puritan practices and family structures as Horton Davies brings attention to the Puritan motto, "Every house a household of faith; every father a priest in his own family."[30] Puritan minister Oliver Heywood, in his influential work *The Family Altar*, equates the role of father to the work of a priest during the Old Testament period. For Heywood, this priestly work included the biblical instruction from Deuteronomy 6:7, "you shall teach [these things] diligently to your children," instructing the people in knowledge (Malachi 2:7), intercessory prayer and confession on behalf of the family for the pardon of sins, personal consecration before the Lord, and prayers of blessing on the household, which describes David's actions for his family in 2 Samuel 6:20.[31] The priestly role of fathers is an active role requiring commitment, faithfulness, and carefulness. Heywood's work in *The Family Altar* also provides ten practical suggestions for fathers to lead their families in family worship. Here are his suggestions summarized: (1) commit to attending a local church that teaches the whole counsel of the Word of God and relies upon the power of the Holy Spirit, (2) study and search the Scriptures to be strong in prayer, (3) from the heart, pray the Lord's prayer and develop and expand personal prayer from its principles, (4) discuss matters of faith with like-minded Christians in community and be willing both to teach and learn from fellow Christians, (5) devote to personal prayer and devotion so that family worship is active and fruitful, (6) study the nature of sin and practice confession, (7) study personal and familial needs and make faithful supplication, (8) write down God's mercy through answered prayers, (9) consider the daily dangers surrounding the family and pray, and (10) plead for the Holy Spirit to be active in the family.[32] These are such helpful suggestions that pastor's today can teach and encourage the fathers in their congregation to think through and apply.

Richard Baxter

The most helpful Puritan to parse out the responsibilities of the father is Pastor Richard Baxter (c.1615–1691). In his work *A Christian Directory*, Baxter devotes a large section for family worship and fathers entitled "Christian Economics." The head of the household is fundamental in Baxter's theology, and his writing assigns the responsibility to men to carry out their God-given authority in the home as non-negotiable. Baxter encourages fathers to devote themselves first to private prayers daily, suggesting personal soul care is first important for the father so he may provide ministry to his family.

Baxter particularly charged fathers to teach their children the Scriptures and how to read them. He suggested this through teaching children to learn the Scriptures by memory through catechizing, and for fathers to provide helpful applications for their children as they lead them. He also provided specific directives and motives to men and parents that are still helpful for today.

In this we have modernized the language as you can see below:

Chapter VIII. *Direct.* VI: The husband must be the principal teacher of the family. He must instruct them, and examine them, and rule them about the matters of God, as well as his own service, and see that the Lord's day and worship be observed by all that are within his gates. And therefore, he must [labor] for such understanding and ability as is necessary hereunto. And if he is unable or negligent, it is his sin, and will be his shame. If the wife be wiser and abler, and it be cast upon her, it is his [dishonor]; but if neither of them do it, the sin, and shame, and suffering, will be common to them both.

Chapter VIII. *Direct.* VII: The husband is to be the mouth of the family, in their daily conjunct prayers unto God. Therefore, he must be able to pray, and also have a praying heart. He must be as it were the priest of the household; and therefore, should be the most holy, that he may be fit to stand between them and God, and to offer up their prayers to Him. If this be cast on the wife, it is his [dishonor].

Chapter X. *Direct.* V. [Labor] much to possess [your children's] hearts with the fear of God, and a reverence for the holy Scriptures, and then whatsoever duty you command them, or whatsoever sin you forbid them, show them some plain and urgent texts of Scripture for it; and cause them to learn them and repeat them.

Chapter X. *Direct.* VI. In all your speeches of God and of Jesus Christ, and of the holy Scripture, or the life to come, or of any holy duty, speak always with gravity, seriousness, and reverence, as of the most great and dreadful and sacred things: for before children come to have any distinct understanding of particulars, it is a hopeful beginning to have their hearts possessed with a general reverence and high esteem for holy matters.

Baxter's focus on exhorting men proves particularly useful for this book. Baxter dedicates chapter five in "Christian Economics" to recommending motives that ought to enthuse men in the faithful leading of their households. Below is the summation of each of Baxter's ten motives:

Motive. I. The family is a considerable part of God's own government in the world. If fathers are not governing their families on behalf of the Lord, then Satan will govern the family.

Motive. II. Consider that in an ungodly, ungoverned family, continued temptation to live in sin exists all the time. Conversely, in a godly, governed family, provocations for a holy life exist. Thus, even if a family member is weak in the faith, the godly structure around can persuade the weak toward godliness.

Motive. III. The godly family lives with God's law ruling principally and teach daily mysteries of the kingdom, open the Scriptures, and lead children to the paths of life. Men make their recreation to know God and to speak of heavenly things always, recognizing their own propensity toward sin.

Motive. IV. The godly family tends to make a holy posterity for generations to come. Thus, the father's daily activity of establishing a godly household has their future lineage in mind.

Motive. V. A well-governed family is preparation for a well-governed church as fathers prepare their children for congregational living through instruction, catechizing, ex-

amination and overseeing. This makes for healthy churches
and more delightful pastoral ministry.

Motive. VI. A well-governed family tends to produce
faithful saints in vocational settings. Consider how to bless
the world with a well-prepared child wherever God ordains
him or her to serve.

Motive. VII. Consider that in a family well-governed,
even if persecution occurs, the church would still meet, as
holy men are prepared to lead their families where pastors
can no longer.

Motive. VIII. The godly man must consider, that even if
scorned by the ungodly for his righteous life and holy gover-
nance of his family, the Scripture obliges this diligent charge.

Motive. IX. The well-governed home is honorable and ex-
emplary to others, that even the ungodly tolerate them with
a certain revere.

Motive. X. God blesses the godly family with a special
presence and favor. They are His churches where He is worshiped, His houses where He dwells, and He engages these
families with love and through the covenants He has made to
them. These families allow Christ to lead them.

Baxter is furthermore helpful in differentiating between worship that
took place in the home and the worship reserved only for the congregation. For example, family worship did not involve partaking in the
Lord's Supper or baptism; Baxter reserved these two ordinances only
for congregational gatherings. For pastors today, this distinction helps
clarify where a father's responsibility as the priest of the home ends
in relation to the pastor or minister's responsibility to the church as a

whole. Baxter's precision in the role of fathers helps create a mindset and philosophy for fathers and can certainly be useful for pastors equipping fathers today.

Other Historical Influences and Practices

J. W. Alexander

With family worship common practice in churches throughout the United Kingdom and the United States in the 17th and 18th centuries, history shows that by the mid-19th century, family worship began to decline. In response to the decline, a Presbyterian minister from New York by the name of J. W. Alexander (c. 1804–1859) wrote of the importance of family worship in his own life in a work he named *Thoughts on Family Worship*. Alexander's book is a helpful treatise for us to consider today as, similar to his day, many Christians in modern times have simply not made family worship a consistent practice. In the preface of his book, Alexander writes, "In a period when the world is every day making new inroads on the church, it has especially invaded the household … There are many heads of families, communicants in our churches, (and according to a credible report) some ruling elders and deacons, who maintain no stated daily service of God in their dwellings."[33] Alexander wanted to fortify families with God's Word as the world continued to gain ground in the church. His work both encourages and convicts, and he serves as a good example of a more recent pastor who was dealing with the moral decay of society infiltrating the Christian home.

Alexander's Nine Objections

Perhaps most helpful in Alexander's work are the nine objections he lists, which state reasons fathers do not lead in family worship. Despite being written in the nineteenth century, his objections remain prevalent for today's fathers and could help pastor's in preparing fathers to lead in family worship. In the last chapter of *Thoughts on Family Worship*, Alexander challenges heads of households with this: "Laying aside all flattering words, we may say plainly, that we regard the neglect of family worship as springing from lukewarmness and worldliness in religion … Where piety is ardent and operative, it cannot but diffuse itself through the domestic structure."[34] We have summarized in more plain words these common objections in Alexander's day against practicing family worship, with Alexander's rebuttals included. These reasons are still common amongst us.

Objection 1: The family service is a dull formality, and our home does well without it.

Rebuttal 1: You have seen family worship performed under great neglect and by irreligious people. Family worship is simple, but in the household of the righteous, it shines with attractions.

Objection 2: Family worship is a fine practice, but it does not fall in line with the customs of this home or its guests.

Rebuttal 2: If the custom of the home is irregular and delayed waking in the morning throughout the household with late nights at the theatre, then family worship will not be the custom of the home.

Objection 3: I have no time to lead in family worship.

Rebuttal 3: Take time to consider your preference for money and the busyness of your vocation over the Lord. The Lord's commands do not contradict one another.

Objection 4: My family is too small.

Rebuttal 4: "Where two or more are gathered ... (Matthew 18:19, 20)."

Objection 5: My family is too large with others living with us, and guests are common.

Rebuttal 5: If your family is large, all the more reason to begin family worship. The more you delay, more people are neglected. Have courage to lead, because "them that honor me, I will honor (1 Samuel 2:30)."

Objection 6: People in my home have greater intelligence in the knowledge of God than I do.

Rebuttal 6: If true, the one with more knowledge in the home should encourage the effort of the head of the household to lead in family worship, knowing the authority God has granted.

Objection 7: I am unlearned, and I do not have spiritual gifts.

Rebuttal 7: Do not add complexity to family worship. Read Scripture and put a few thoughts together for your family. The one who aids in your personal devotion will aid the family in worship.

Objection 8: My family is unwilling to participate.

Rebuttal 8: Assert your authority in the divine role given to you by the Lord and faithfully lead your home. An unwilling older child further proves that beginning family worship early is best.

Objection 9: I am ashamed of who I am. I cannot lead my family, for I fear their thoughts of me.

Rebuttal 9: This is the most common objection, more powerful than the others combined. Do not be ashamed of Christ, and do not balk at the test of the sincerity of your faith.[35]

These objections and rebuttals are for men to consider and take before the Lord. The objections are not meant to discourage, but to edify, convict, and apply. Mutual encouragement amongst the fathers in the same congregation to remain faithful and accountable to their responsibilities is necessary and recognizing objections can help cauterize inactivity.

Conclusion on the Historical Practices of Family Worship

There are several key principles from history and the practices of individuals are essential for equipping. Throughout much of church history, the great influencers of family worship have viewed the home as a "little church." John Chrysostom and Augustine, continuing with Luther, the Puritans, Matthew Henry, and Jonathan Edwards all viewed the home as a continuation of the church and emphasized the importance of the home within the kingdom of God. Creating this mindset and philosophy in the paternal culture of your congregation will only strengthen fathers to carry out personal and family devotion, which will ultimately strengthen the church as a whole by creating a new culture. We as pastors should continue to emphasize that the church is not a building but rather a people, and wherever the Lord's people gather, teaching of Scripture and responsive worship can occur.

Emerging also from this chapter are examples and exhortations throughout history of the responsibility fathers and heads of households have to their families. God has entrusted fathers with the duty to train their children in the Scriptures, and fathers should diligently carry out this work. The order is important, however, as fathers must first participate in personal study and prayer in secret to prepare themselves for intentional leading of their families. This concept connects nicely with the idea introduced in Deuteronomy 6, which encourages parents to know "these things" first in their hearts and then to teach them diligently to their children.

These first two chapters have attempted to confirm both in the Scripture, and the application of the Scripture throughout the Church's history, that heads of households are to teach God's Word. Later in chapter 4, we will consider some helpful practices for teaching fathers to study God's Word, both for themselves and for their families. Many men do not read the Scriptures, much less teach the Scriptures, and we as pastors must prepare them to do what God has asked of them.

Endnotes

[1] Coleman, Lyman. *The Antiquities of the Christian Church* (Andover, MA; New York, NY: Gould, Newman & Saxton, 1841).

[2] *Didache* 4.9. Also known as *The Teaching of the Twelve Apostles*, the *Didache* is considered to be dated in the later part of the first century or beginning of the second century. Christian tradition credits the sources to the twelve apostles as a sort of book of order as the early church was being established.

[3] Kerry Ptacek, *Family Worship: Biblical Basis, Historical Reality, Current Need* (Birmingham, AL: Covenant Family Fellowship, 1994), 40.

[4] Polycarp and the Church at Smyrna, *Polycarp's Letter to the Philippians & His Martyrdom: The Early Christians*, 4.2.

[5] Tertullian, *Ad Uxorem* ("To my wife"), bk. 2, ch. 8; available through "The Tertullian Project," http://www.tertullian.org/works/ad_uxorem.htm.

[6] Coleman, *The Antiquities of the Christian Church*, 379.

[7] Philip Schaff, *History of the Christian Church: Nicene and Post-Nicene Christianity, From Constantine the Great to Gregory the Great*, vol. 3 (New York, NY: Charles Scribner's Sons, 1891), 545. Ptacek credits Chrysostom as a witness to the continued view of male headship in the home up to this point in church history. See Ptacek, *Family Worship*, 40.

[8] Schaff, *History of the Church*, 545.

[9] Jeffrey C. Robinson, Sr., "The Home is an Earthly Kingdom," *JDFM* 3.1 (2012): 18.

[10] Ibid., 19-20.

[11] *The Book of Concord: Concordia Triglotta Edition* published in 1917. Trans. by F. Bente and W.H.T. Dau.

[12] Robinson, Sr., "The Home is an Earthly Kingdom," 20.

[13] John Calvin, *Harmony of Exodus, Leviticus, Numbers, Deuteronomy: Calvin's Commentaries, Vol. II,* trans. Charles William Bingham, repr. (Grand Rapids, MI: Baker Books, 2009), 366.

[14] Alexander, J. W. *Thoughts on Family Worship* (London, Edinburgh, New York: Nelson, Paternoster Row, 1847. Repr., Location: Andersite, 2017), 200.

[15] Ibid., 201-202. The Presbyteries would also ask heads of households if local elders visited their home quarterly to ask these questions.

[16] Whitney, Donald S. *Family Worship* (Wheaton, IL: Crossway, 2016), 32.

[17] *The Books of Discipline, and of Common Order: The Directory for Family Worship; The Form of Process; And the Order of Election of Superintendents, Ministers, Elders, and Deacons* (Repr. London: Forgotten Books, 2015), 9.

[18] Ibid., Section I.

[19] Ibid., Sections I, II, III.

[20] Ibid., Section IV.

[21] *The 1689: The Second London Baptist Confession* 22:6. The same quote is mentioned in the *Westminster Confession of Faith* 21:6.

[22] *The 1689: The Second London Baptist Confession, Preface: To the Judicious and Impartial Reader.*

[23] Leland Ryken, *Worldly Saints: The Puritans as They Really Were* (Grand Rapids, MI: Zondervan, 1986), 73.

[24] Matthew Henry, *A Church in the House*, repr. (Minneapolis, MN: Curiosmith Bookshop, 2017), 11.

[25] Ryken, Leland. *Worldly Saints: The Puritans as They Really Were*, 75.

[26] Davies, Horton. *The Worship of the English Puritans*. Repr. (Morgan, PA: Soli Deo Gloria, 1997), 278.

[27] Ibid., 278-279.

[28] Edmund S. Morgan, *The Puritan Family: Religion & Domestic Relations in Seventeenth-Century New England*, repr. (Mansfield Centre, CT: Martino, 2014), 45-46.

[29] Ibid., 46.

[30] Davies, *The Worship of English Puritans*, 282.

[31] Oliver Heywood, *The Family Altar*, vol. 4, repr. (Morgan, PA: Soli Deo Gloria, 1999), 309-311. Permission granted on 6/1/21.

[32] Ibid., 378-390.

[33] Alexander, *Thoughts on Family Worship*, 189.

[34] Ibid., 331.

[35] Ibid., 331-337.

CHAPTER 3

Overview of the Elements of Family Worship

This chapter discusses three practical ways that worship can be expressed in the home. Though worshiping God can be displayed in all that one does, building the practice within the family is not to be over complicated. We focus this chapter on the elements of reading, praying, and singing in the family and how these elements lead the family to love and consider God together and teach how parents and children, as individuals, can worship the Lord.

Elements and Practices of Family Worship

Revisiting Deuteronomy 6 again, verse 7 reminds parents that our instruction and worship ought to take place at all times and in every place, "You shall teach them [God's Word] diligently to your children, and shall talk of them when you sit in your house, and when you walk by the way, and when you lie down, and when you rise." There ought to be no dichotomies to our worship, nor our instruction. Our instruction and leading in worship as parents should not merely be limited to one location with our children. Rather our instruction and worship should permeate all areas of our lives. Christ is the King of the cosmos, all authority in Heaven and on earth has been given to Him (Matthew 28:18), and this declaration includes our lives, our time, our resources, our children, and our time with our children.

That said, where do we begin this type of culture in our families? We must begin somewhere as Christians, as to do nothing is to sin since God has instructed His people with imperatives. So, where can we faithfully begin? What practices can we commence in our homes that can lead to our families knowing God and worshiping God?

Let's first identify basic elements of worship. We believe, along with several other pastors and scholars, that the biblical and most practical elements of family worship are *reading and teaching the Scriptures*, *praying*, and *singing/worship*.[1] Though these elements clearly connect with applications given in Scripture, the elements together do not explicitly tie to one particular passage. However, the records available of the early church help solidify the individual elements uniformly applied to household worship. Coleman describes families assembling early in the morning for a reading from an Old Testament passage, followed by a hymn, and finished by prayer and supplication.[2] Early Christians repeated hymns and melodies of the sacred songs sung during family worship over the course of the day in private and throughout the places of employment for each family member to "cheer themselves" of the song's sentiments.[3] These family gatherings featured thoughtful prayer. The families praised the Lord for preserving the family throughout the night, thanked the Lord for their physical and mental health and His goodness to allow them to meet together for worship, and petitioned the Lord to keep them from temptation throughout the day and for the ability to walk out their lives in a worthy manner.[4]

Though not all family worship resources emphasize the same elements, for simplicity and effectiveness, we are highlighting three basic elements of family worship: reading/teaching Scripture, praying, and singing praise unto the Lord. These fundamental practices are meant to encourage daily commitment to both personal worship and family worship in the home. These elements are to be implemented because they are good and they can help facilitate worship, but even more than that, they are opportunities for us to know God, praise God, and talk to

God. God, Himself, is the treasure of these practices. He is the focus of our worship. He is the hope for our lives.

Over the next three chapters, one category at a time, we will examine practices to help further implement these elements in family worship. We want to identify these practices, learn how better to steward them, and then apply the elements in our homes and throughout our congregations because Christ is worthy of the praise.

Endnotes

[1] Whitney, *Family Worship*, 44. Marcellino, Jerry. *Rediscovering Family Worship* (Wapwallopen, PA: Shepherd Press, 2011), 15-18.

[2] Coleman, *Antiquities of the Christian Church*, 375.

[3] Ibid.

[4] Ibid.

PART 2

WALK THE ANCIENT PATHS

CHAPTER 4

Equipping Fathers for Personal Worship Through Scripture Study

Chapter four discusses the need for fathers to study God's Word, that they may know God, and grow in their love for God. This chapter provides simple hermeneutical practices and questions for the father to utilize when engaging God's Word. The practices are meant to help fathers grow personally in the faith, so they are equipped and prepared to lead their families in the praise and worship of God.

Scripture

God's Word, as we have said, is the bedrock for guiding all our worship and praise of God. Alexander, in *Thoughts on Family Worship*, believed daily Bible reading is an indispensable piece to family worship, which one should not omit for anything.[1] Alexander fastened this indispensability to the conviction that God's Word appointed family instruction in Deuteronomy 6:7-9, having the household's future faithfulness in mind with all of God's people having access to His Word.[2] Alexander's practical components of Scripture reading had the head of the household reading it the length and depth of explanation after reading the passage based on the gifts of each officiant, the length of the passage and selection determined by the head of household, and the whole Bible as eligible for reading in family worship.

As we have discussed, before we lead family worship, one must know the One Whom he is leading his family to. Fathers are called to know God first. Remember what Moses said in Deuteronomy 6, *"You shall love the LORD your God with all your heart and with all your soul and with all your might. And these words that I command you today shall be on your heart. You shall teach them diligently to your children ..."* We love God first, with our entire being, and *then* we teach our children. A father must ask himself a very important question: *Do I love God? Do I know God?* He has given us His Word, and the Word reveals who God is.

It is possible for a man to read the Scriptures aimlessly. But this is not what God intended. He wants us to know Him. And He wants us to proclaim Him and His good news. He wants us to learn and grow in the mystery of Christ that He has revealed to us (Ephesians 3:4-6).

Reading the Scriptures

We want this chapter to focus on reading (and teaching) the Scriptures in a God-centered way as opposed to reading the Scriptures with man as the center-view... or even an aimless reading. If we do so, we will enjoy God for all that He is, and all that He has done for us. As well, we will learn the appropriate place of man in the story of redemption as revealed in Scripture.

These practical and helpful questions will help fathers understand the passages of Scripture they read. Provide these questions to the men in your church to help them interpret the Bible correctly.

Approaching the Scriptures with God in mind (hermeneutical questions):

1. What does this passage tell me about God? (Who He is: character, promises, covenants, love, attributes, etc.)
2. Who of the Trinity is the text describing (Father, Son, Spirit)? And what is His/Their role?

3. How does the text point us to the person and work of Christ?

4. What comfort do you find knowing what the text says of God?

5. What does the text say about our response, or responsibility?

6. How does this text remind us that we are not God, but need God?

7. What does this passage tell us about ourselves? Our sinful inclination?

8. What does this passage tell us about what God desires from us?

9. How is God able to help us accomplish what He desires for us?

10. Why does God want us to know what He is revealing from the text we are studying?

Notice that these questions help us think about God first before we deal with our own hearts, circumstances, sin, and obedience. Our natural inclination when we read the Bible is to think about what we are supposed to do. However, before we know what to do, let us consider who God is. His glory should seize us. His love should motivate us to want to love and obey in response. So often we pass over God Himself. Our strong encouragement: do not pass over the Lord. Linger in your thoughts about Him.

Let's Practice!

Example of a God-Centered Hermeneutic:

Matthew 28:18-20 The Great Commission (certainly you can answer more to each question):

1. **What does this passage tell me about God? (Who He is: character, promises, covenants, love, attributes, etc.)**

- All authority in Heaven and on earth has been given to Jesus (v. 18). (Who else in history can say such a thing!)
- Jesus promises to be with His people to the end of the earth (v. 20).
- His authority is the very reason and motive for His disciples to "Go" (v. 18).

2. **Who of the Trinity is the text describing (Father, Son, Spirit)? And what is His/Their role?**
   - Jesus, God the Son, is describing Himself as the One having authority on Heaven and earth (v. 18).
   - The Name that all are to be baptized into is God the Father, God the Son, and God the Holy Spirit. Three persons, One God, mentioned in the glorious text (v. 19). Salvation belongs fully to our God!

3. **How does the text point us to the person and work of Christ?**
   - He has all authority (v. 18).
   - Including the authority to tell us to "Go" on His behalf (v. 19).
   - He has revealed His teaching through His Word (v. 20).
   - He has a heart for all nations to be saved (v. 19).
   - He will care for His people to the very end (v. 20).

4. **What comfort do you find knowing what the text says of God?**
   - That our God has authority and concern over all nations (v. 19).
   - That He knows we need Him to be with us and to help us in our "going" (v. 20).

5. **What does the text say about our response, or responsibility?**
   - One imperative: make disciples of all nations (v. 19).
   - Three participles: go, baptize, and teach (v. 19-20).

- To trust Him that He will in fact be with us as we make disciples (v. 20).
- To yield to Him as King over Heaven and earth (v. 18).

6. **How does this text remind us that we are not God, but need God?**
   - Very simply, we do not rule heaven or earth, nor anything in them.
   - Our name is not worthy to be baptized in.
   - We do not know what to teach unless God tells us.
   - Even our disciple-making cannot occur apart from God's work.
   - We are fully dependent upon our Great God and King.

7. **What does this passage tell us about ourselves? Our sinful inclination?**
   - That we do have responsibility in God's Kingdom.
   - That all men need to obey God by being baptized and taught God's Word.
   - That God's truth does not discriminate against our ethnicity.
   - We need to hear the gospel, and so do others, because we are sinful and need the saving grace of God.

8. **What does this passage tell us about what God desires from us?**
   - That we would make disciples in His Name.
   - That we, and others, would obey Him.
   - That we, and others, would be baptized in His name (confessing, repenting, and appealing).
   - That we would point the nations to the King!

9. **How is God able to help us accomplish what He desires for us?**
   - When He has all authority, that means there is no authority left to gain. He is the Sovereign and King over all things in every part of creation.

- He knows we cannot accomplish the task of making disciples, or obeying Him, apart from Himself. So, He promises to be with us in this work. (What encouragement!)

10. **Why does God want us to know what He is revealing from the text we are studying?**
    - Because He wants us to be a part of His plan to bring glory to the Son.
    - He has had a heart for the nations first revealed in Genesis 12:3, and Jesus is the means and end to accomplishing His love for the nations.
    - He wants us to know the Son and the victory He has in His resurrection.

Asking the questions listed above for this text (Matthew 28) emphasizes God's role in our disciple making. He is the Great authority of the cosmos. His work is the true and deep work behind everything possible.

What if we approached the text without considering God from the text? The approach would then be in contrast to what we've just done in Matthew 28:18-20. In reading the text, it is fairly easy to see that Christians are supposed to make disciples. But knowing we are commissioned to make disciples, but not considering that Christ has all authority, or that He is always with us in our disciple making, puts a tremendous burden on our backs—a burden we cannot carry. We must rest in the gospel. We must rest in the work of Christ on our behalf. We must realize our dependence on Him. If we forget these truths about God, and we go out making disciples without resting in His work and power, then we have adapted a man-centered work ethic and man-centered hermeneutic, and ultimately, it could lead to a man-centered dependence.

In Scripture, the *indicative* (Who God is, what He has done), is always more important than the *imperative* (what we are supposed to do in obedience). Both are important. Both are essential. But the indicative is more important because it reveals God and His work. We want to be

God-centered men, so we can teach God-centered things to our children. This is very important in family worship.

Let's Practice Again!

Another example from Isaiah 53:

1. **What does this passage tell me about God? (Who He is: character, promises, covenants, love, attributes, etc.)**
   - In Isaiah 53, we have a description of the Suffering Servant (Jesus) who is God's Son. The Lord wants to reveal Himself to us (verse 1). He loves us so much that He is willing to sacrifice His Son for our redemption (verse 10).

2. **Who of the Trinity is the text describing (Father, Son, Spirit)? And what is His/Their role?**
   - The passage focuses on the sacrifice of the Messiah for all of mankind's sins. As a servant who was humble in appearance (verse 2) and behavior (verse 7), He accepted the humiliation (verse 3) and the brutality (verses 3-10) of the cross so we can know peace and restoration (verse 5).

3. **How does the text point us to the person and work of Christ?**
   - In addition to the points made in #2, He died on our behalf (verses 8-9). He served as a sacrificial offering—a justification for many and He carried our iniquities (verse 11).

4. **What comfort do you find knowing what the text says of God?**
   - While I am in rebellion, Jesus died on my behalf and bore my sins (verse 12).

5. **What does the text say about our response, or responsibility?**
   - Mankind despised the Savior and did not value Him (verse 3). He was pierced for our transgressions (verse 5).

6. **How does this text remind us that we are not God, but need God?**
   - "By his knowledge shall the righteous one, my servant, make many to be accounted righteous, and he shall bear their iniquities" (verse 11). The text is clear that God demanded something I cannot do for myself. Only the Savior's sacrifice will suffice for my sin.

7. **What does this passage tell us about ourselves? Our sinful inclination?**
   - We all went astray like sheep, and we all turned to our own way (verse 6). Each of us is considered one of the rebels in verse 12.

8. **What does this passage tell us about what God desires from us?**
   - There are no "imperatives" in this passage, that is, things we must do in response to the Savior's sacrifice. [This illustrates that not every one of these ten questions will be answered in every text.]

9. **How is God able to help us accomplish what He desires for us?**
   - He wants us to know peace (verse 5). He was willing to punish His Son for my sin (verse 6) and present Him as restitution for each one of us (verse 10).

10. **Why does God want us to know what He is revealing from the text we are studying?**
    - He wants us to be aware of the cost of our freedom and restoration that He presents to us in Jesus.

Sometimes the passage you are studying may be unclear in some of the details or even the main idea. Here are some additional questions that may help you unravel a confusing verse:

Who is the author? In the case of our illustration from Isaiah 53, the author was a prophet that lived in Jerusalem and began his prophetic ministry around 730 BC. These details are important for understanding chapter 53. This section is clearly a foretelling of future events. He spoke them in his lifetime, but these words would be an encouragement to the Jewish people who were carried into exile by the Babylonians in 586 BC. Isaiah received a prophetic vision from God for both the time period of the exile and the coming of Jesus over 700 years in the future.

To whom is the author writing? Just like Paul wrote special letters for unique purposes to different churches, Isaiah spoke to God's people during a season of rebellion and unfaithfulness, particularly in the case of the Northern Kingdom. The Southern Kingdom, for which Jerusalem was the capital, would make much needed changes, but then lapse back into idolatry. His audience was well acquainted with God's displeasure, His expectations for Godliness, and His decision for judgment.

What is the situation and situations throughout the book or passage? The Gospels were written by eyewitnesses of the life of Christ. Paul wrote most of his letters to recipients with whom he had spent time and many whom he led to faith in Christ. Isaiah wrote to a generation of citizens of Jerusalem who watched the Northern Kingdom fail miserably and be punished severely at the hands of the Assyrians. They recognized, at least for a season, rebellion has harsh consequences.

How did the original audience understand the meaning? Like viewing a mountain range from a distance, the spectator can identify peaks in the distance, but he will have difficulty judging the distance between individual peaks. So too, these hearers in Jerusalem would not have identified or understood the prophecy about the Suffering Servant with the same clarity that present-day believers have.

Why is the context important? In the case of the Gospels, eyewitness accounts of the risen Lord give important credibility to His resurrection. Paul was exhorting new believers, not in a vacuum, but in a special context that often-needed immediate correction. Isaiah gave extensive prophecies to his listeners whose grandchildren and great grandchildren would need to rehearse during their time in exile.

Are there parallel passages in other books that support and clarify the meaning of the verses you are studying? Isaiah is the Old Testament book that is most often cited in the Gospels. Chapter 53:9 is fulfilled when Jesus is buried in the tomb of Joseph of Arimathea (Luke 23:50-56). Matthew quotes 53:4 to highlight Jesus' fulfillment of that prophecy. Psalm 22 is a familiar Old Testament passage that predicted the brutal sacrifice of our Savior.

These are simply questions and suggestions for you to apply to your own personal study and worship of God, first. We are to be people who worship our amazing God and marvel at what has been revealed to us, about Himself, through His Word. And then we have the joy and privilege to teach those in our homes about Him. And to teach them the tools to study for themselves our Great God. In studying God's Word, we learn God. When we teach His Word, we teach about God.

Here are some helpful resources we recommend in addition to these very basic instructions:

40 Questions About Interpreting the Bible by Robert L. Plummer

How to Read the Bible for All its Worth by Gordon Fee

Biblical Theology: How the Church Faithfully Teaches the Gospel by Nick Roark and Robert Cline

For the sake of your own heart and for your families, consume God's Word as your daily appetite. Jeremiah the prophet said, "Your words were found, and I ate them, and your words became to me a joy and the delight of my heart, for I am called by your name, O LORD, God of hosts (Jeremiah 15:16)." He "ate" the Word and then the Word became a joy and delight to him. May the Lord fill us with the hope and truth of His Word for His glory.

Endnotes

[1] Alexander, *Thoughts on Family Worship*, 305.

[2] Ibid., 312-313.

CHAPTER 5

Equipping Fathers for Leading Prayer

This chapter will discuss some practical ways for fathers to engage in prayer with their families. We examine the ACTS prayer paradigm, biblical commands, and historical and modern useful prayer models to implement in family worship. This chapter also discusses the necessity for children to learn to pray by hearing their fathers (and parents) pray. Another important aspect of this chapter is connecting prayer with ministries and missions in the local church.

This story is a tough one to share, but I will set aside my pride and admit my weaknesses. I (Ken) love to cut grass and made a major investment—a zero turn riding lawn mower. Actually, I thought I knew enough about lawn mowers and lawn maintenance to be able to handle this incredible machine. I was wrong.

The delivery man backed it off the trailer, gave me a quick demo, and left for his next delivery. I climbed aboard and tested it out. Slowly accelerating, I inched along unaccustomed to a moving vehicle that had no pedals! No brake pedal to stop. No gas pedal to accelerate. It's all in your hands. Thankfully I missed my wife's car on this maiden voyage. After jerking and swerving, I got it safely parked in the garage.

Where it sat for two months.

This amazing tool went unused while the grass grew week after week. Then I decided to contact a family friend who agreed to talk me through it and demonstrate driving my zero turn. One afternoon he talked me through a new way of driving a riding lawn mower. Then he demonstrated it for me while he cut the backyard. Finally, he watched me finish the yard, coaching and encouraging me all the way through the process. In less than a half hour I had a new mental framework and a new positive attitude.

Now I use the mower almost weekly, and I do so almost effortlessly. Steering the powerful machine has become second nature. Gone is the uncertainty and anxiety. It has become my favorite tool and a significant time saver.

Now, in case you are wondering if this is a sales pitch for the latest in lawn equipment, it is not. But I share the story to illustrate the hurdles you and your family may have to overcome before each member becomes comfortable with the powerful discipline of prayer. Secondly, we want you to get a vision for how the Lord can use you in the life of your children to model, coach, and encourage as they grow in their appreciation for how the Lord wishes each one of His created children to communicate with Him.

Prayer

Why is prayer important?

Praying as a family is both a blessing and a responsibility. We want to be men and leaders who pray *for* our families, pray *with* our families, and teach our families *how to* pray. As seen in Ephesians 6:4, we are to be priests in the home: instructors and interceders. Fathers pray for their families (both alone, and with them). Fathers lovingly pray for their families just as Christ lovingly intercedes for us (Hebrews 5:1-2; 7:23-27). We are priests in this way, similar to how Christ is for us. God has asked us to pray without ceasing (1 Thessalonians 5:16-18), and He has commanded us to train and instruct our children, therefore we must carry over the call to pray without ceasing for those we instruct.

We pray for our families because we ought to be men of prayer, priestly in nature. Think of it this way, if you are not praying for your family, then who is? We pray for them to love God, to know God, to be aware of their sin, to confess and repent, to have faith, to love the nations, to honor their parents, to love the Church, etc. We appeal to God on their behalf. Just as Christ appeals to the Father for His church (John 17:1-17; Hebrews 7:25). We pray because we have reason to praise God, thank God, confess our sins to Him, and pray for our needs and the needs of others.

We pray with our families so our families will be marked by the Spirit of God through family prayer. We get to enjoy God and praise Him together, we thank God for all we have in Christ and monetary provisions, we confess and are open about our brokenness and desperate need for God. And we pray for our needs, the church, the lost around us, missionaries, our country, and all the other matters surrounding us. Prayer helps create the language for the whole house to operate in.

And in this act, we teach our sons and daughters to pray. We teach them how to rejoice in God, and praise His name, and depend upon Him for forgiveness and provision and salvation. We teach our children to pray in His name. Is there any gift better that parents could provide their children than teaching them to depend on, rejoice in, and pray to the Almighty God? Is there anything better than to have an intimate relationship with Him afforded through prayer? There is not. The discipline of personal prayer and devotion to God leads to healthy and faithful corporate prayer in the family. These practical tools listed below are meant to provide ideas for praying in the home, both personally and within the family.

Before we proceed, it is important to note we need God's help to pray. We do not muster up affections or inclinations for the things of God without the work of God. Our joy is to abide in God, and His Word abides in us (John 15:7). We appeal to God in prayer (Matthew 6:9), we trust the Spirit intercedes on our behalf (Romans 8:26-27), and Christ prays for us (Hebrews 7:25). Every suggestion and discipline listed below must first run through the truth that God is working in us through prayer. Our prayer must be God-centered.

Though not explicitly mentioned in Deuteronomy 6:4-9 or Ephesians 6:4, prayer is an important part of the Christian life as seen throughout Scripture, thus why would it not be a part of family worship? Oliver Heywood wrote, "God bids us pray without ceasing, in all places, in every kind of prayer, and leaves it to prudence for particular places, times, words, and associates, so that it answers the main of God's glory, communion with Him, and edification. Let not copious wits raise disputes to make void the substance of duty, because the circumstance is not expressed."[1] Family worship, therefore, creates another opportunity to pray unto the Lord together as a family.

We teach our children to pray in the name of Jesus who redeemed us back to fellowship with God. We teach our children how to pray and what to pray, as they are learning from us and will emulate our practices. In praying as a family, therefore, fathers not only have the responsibility to pray and intercede for their children, like the priestly role espoused by Puritans as discussed previously, but also the added responsibility of teaching children how to pray and what to pray for. Children hearing their fathers plead for their souls, as they learn of the humility to confess sin, and observe what it means to praise and glorify Christ creates a glorious culture in the home.

Helpful Prayer Tools:

The familiar ACTS paradigm is a helpful tool for biblical prayers. Simply put, the ACTS paradigm focuses on four categories of prayer: *Adoration, Confession, Thanksgiving,* and *Supplication.* Perhaps this paradigm below will be helpful:

- **A**doration: Praising God for Who He is
  Psalm 145; Matthew 6:9
- **C**onfession: Stating sin, and asking forgiveness
  Psalm 51; 1 John 1:9
- **T**hanksgiving: Thanking God for specific things He has done
  Psalm 107:8-9; 1 Timothy 4:4-5; 1 Thessalonians 5:18
- **S**upplication: Asking God for things we want and need
  Matthew 6:11; Luke 11:9-12

It is a helpful practice to run through Scripture and gather truth that belongs under each of the ACTS categories and then to pray for those things. As a very simple example, we have selected the Lord's Prayer in Matthew 6:9-13 to walk through. Now, just like all helpful tools, we still need to rely on the Spirit in our prayers. God help us to pray!

Matthew 6:9-13:

Adoration/Praise:

- v. 9 "Our Father in Heaven, Hallowed be Your Name"

Confession:

- v. 12 "Forgive us our debts, as we also forgive our debtors"

Thanksgiving:

- v. 10 "Your Kingdom come; your will be done"

Supplication:

- v. 11 "Give us today our daily bread"; v. 13 "Lead us not into temptation but deliver us from evil"

The Lord's Prayer is worthy to be prayed! It teaches us our posture before Him, outlines categories for prayer, displays our need for God, identifies our capacity for temptation, and concludes with the song we should all sing—"thy Kingdom come and will be done!"

It's not enough to agree that prayer is a good thing. It wasn't enough for me to purchase an expensive mower. I needed help moving forward. Your children need your help to make progress in their prayer lives. Think about a variety of avenues that you can use to communicate the basics of prayer:

- Read Scripture about prayer aloud.
- Suggest Scripture each child can read, for those who are ready.
- Write a list of things you and your family are praying for.
- Write short prayers in a prayer journal.
- Listen while older children pray.
- Listen while parents pray.
- Give encouragement as each one participates.
- Discuss loving correction in small doses as needed.
- Talk about prayer and listening to God outside of devotions.
- Talk about questions each one may have.
- Remember to discuss answers to prayer.
- Rehearse the basics of prayer.

This list of suggestions is not a magic formula but some practical illustrations of how you lead your family that is consistent with Deuteronomy 6. As both adults and children read, listen, discuss, write, remember, and receive coaching and correction, the Holy Spirit uses all these practices to build strong pathways in our minds that establish durable learning.

For more prayer topics for family worship, here is a list of more suggestions (though not exhaustive):

Pray for Intimacy With God:

- For us to know God, love God, and our affections for God to grow.

- For God's glory in all things (1 Corinthians 10:31).
- Ask for God's help, recognize our complete and utter dependence.
- For our family members to love God, and for their daily needs.
- For our church members, pastors, elders, deacons, and missionaries.
- For the lost: (neighbors by name, nations).

Prayer for Husbands and Wives:

- That we would love God with all heart/soul/mind. That we would praise God and know Him.
- That we would serve/submit to God and one another, and lean upon Him to fulfill our roles (Ephesians 4–6)
- That our marriage is an example of Christ and the church, for the church, and the lost world.
- That we would remain faithful to one another.

Prayer for Parents:

- That our children would love God and serve Him alone (Deuteronomy 11:13b).
- That my parenting may speak truth, that we live what we speak, promoting the fruit of the Spirit in our relationship (Galatians 5:22-23).
- That our children will come to a saving grace of God early in their lives, as Samuel did (1 Samuel 3:20-21).
- That our children will fear God and hate their sin (Psalm 97:10).
- That God will give them a love for His Son's church (Ephesians 2).
- That God will raise up other godly disciple-makers, friends, church leaders, and a spouse made for him or her (2 Timothy 2:2).

- That they will make disciples (Matthew 28:18-20; 2 Timothy 2:2; Titus 2).
- That the children would love God's Word and be contrite in spirit and tremble at His Word (Isaiah 66:2).
- That they would listen to the instruction of their parents and for true biblical wisdom to a close friend (Proverbs 1–9).
- That our children will come under strong conviction when they sin (Create in me a new heart!) (Psalm 51).
- That our children grow in the grace and knowledge of their Lord and Savior Jesus Christ (2 Peter 3:18).
- That they confess their sins to God (1 John 1:9).
- That they confess their sins to the church (James 5:16).
- That our children long for the King's return (1 Peter 4:13).

We would submit to you some really helpful prayer guides for your family worship:

A Praying Life by Paul Miller

A Guide to Prayer by Isaac Watts

A Method for Prayer by Matthew Henry

The Family Worship Book by Terry L. Johnson

To pray for and teach children to pray is better than any Christmas gift we could give them. Let us devote ourselves to this. May we push through when it is difficult or when we do not feel like it. May God be glorified, and our children be blessed.

Endnotes

[1] Heywood, *Family Altar*, 328.

CHAPTER 6

Equipping Fathers for Leading Praise and Singing

As discussed in a previous chapter, the most uncommon element of family worship practiced amongst fathers is singing. This chapter will highlight what it looks like to sing together as a family, how a father can lead a family in singing, and how the Scriptures and history highlight the practice of singing hymns and spiritual songs. Singing with a worshipful response to the glorious deeds of God is the posture of this practice, so helping fathers through the discomfort of singing and encouraging them to sing with their families is the intent behind the chapter.

Singing can be awkward in a family setting. It just can. Especially when gifts of music have not exactly been given to the family. I (Blair) remember my first few attempts to lead in singing during family worship. My five-year-old (at the time) looked at me like, "What are you doing?"

To add injury to insult, my family and I were recently invited over to the home of a very sweet family in our church. After dessert, the husband of the family suggested that we all go into their piano room and sing a hymn together. I loved the idea as our family regularly sings praise songs and hymns together. The song selected was the *Doxology*, which was agreed upon as both of our families sing this song often during family worship. This family happens to be a supremely gifted musical family (the piano room descriptor probably gave that away).

One of their children led us with the piano, and we sang and worshiped together. My family was blown away by their voices, four-part harmony, and musical ability. It was clear to us immediately, the way the two families sing and worship is different. My kids looked up with the expression of "Wow" on their faces!

With that said, I was reminded of a very valuable lesson that night, and so were my wife and kids: God is glorified when our friends sing and worship with their many gifts, and God is glorified when our family sings. God has been worshiped in many ways and with different instruments throughout history, and He is chiefly concerned with the posture of the heart of the worshiper (Romans 15:5-7). God receives the glory due His name when His people sing His praises, no matter the level of musical ability (Psalm 66:2).

Nevertheless, I pushed through the awkwardness. Why? Isn't reading and praying enough? Simply put, God's people were made to praise Him. And singing is a joyous expression of that.

So, God's people sing. This is a significant part of the worship we partake in. Worship is recorded throughout the Psalms as hymns of praise, poems of faith and thanksgiving, and songs of lament and repentance capture the range of human emotions spilled out toward God. In the best days of life and in our hardest seasons, we sing to God. From Mary singing and praising the Lord when she learned she was with child (Luke 1:46-55), to Paul and Silas singing praise to God while sitting in a Roman jail (Acts 16:25), God is glorified when His people respond to Him in worship.

How encouraging it is for us to know that our God, Himself, sings (Zephaniah 3:17). Even observing how Christ sang with His disciples after a meal in Matthew 26:30 (not totally different from what my family did with our friends that night), can provide such a helpful picture of intimate group worship. Christ ends His fellowship time with a song to God, right before He is betrayed. It is powerful to think about. This

King, who was betrayed on our behalf, is worthy to receive the songs of praise He deserves.

Coleman, as has already been referenced, reports that the early church sang hymns in their homes as a part of their worship unto the Lord.[1] Psalm 78 gives the responsibility to fathers to not only instruct their children in the commands of the Lord but also to teach them the "glorious deeds" of the Lord, which can provoke a worshipful response from within. Family worship, therefore, can provide a medium each day to consider the work of the Lord and praise Him for all that He is and has done. Teach your children the glories of God, and they will respond in worship. The songs we select should be inspired by the truth of who God is. Our praises glorify the Lord and encourage and strengthen our families.

J. W. Alexander urged singing in his congregation and described it as the "instated means of giving expression to every high religious emotion."[2] However, singing is not only an emotive experience but also a form of Christian instruction.[3] Thus, what we choose to sing is very important as it should be theologically sound. Singing is instructive and formative. Therefore, we want to sing songs that are true and not just good in melody. Remember, this is how we pass along God's glorious deeds and traits.

Fathers, you might not be the most gifted singer or musician, but you can lead through this initial discomfort and rely upon the Lord to help you. We shouldn't fear one another in our families. We should praise the One we do fear. Worship has a special way of gripping our hearts, seizing our wandering minds, and binding us in agreement.

So how do we begin?

To begin, gather your family and explain to them the blessing of singing to our glorious God and how you desire to sing with them. Address the awkwardness, or any objections, all upfront. Appeal to them to trust you as this is something that will please God and bring life to your family's hearts and devotional times.

Engage Your Family With an Activity:

Write down your family worship hymns and songs as a family and discuss why these songs are meaningful to each person. What Scriptures come to mind with the songs selected? What great truths and promises are in them that encourage your heart? Just having a conversation about your favorite songs can be helpful toward a culture of singing in the house.

There are two principles to operate by in leading worship in the home:

1) The singing and worship must be directed to the Lord.

2) The songs selected and sung should be doctrinally sound and aligned with biblical truths.

Take the opportunity to shepherd your children in these moments. Reframe their hearts as to why they sing and to Whom they sing. Shaping their understanding over and again is our job as a parent. We teach them what they do not yet know, and we model faithfulness for them.

Practical Ideas and Suggestions:

- Purchase a family hymnal or songbook with God-centered hymns (for example: *The Rejoice Hymnal* from Randall House).
- Choose a few hymns that your family knows well (my family calls these battle hymns).
- Learn new songs together and take the time needed to do so.
- If someone reads music, let them assist in the leading of worship.
- If no one plays an instrument, simply sing a cappella (probably how Christ and the disciples sang in Matthew 26).

- If no one plays an instrument, then search for the song online or with a music app with which you can sing along.

- One practice we do in our home is singing songs that the congregation also sings. This has helped our kids tremendously connect home worship with corporate worship and has also helped them feel more comfortable with the song's words as we sing them in two different settings. (Not to mention, it's made my life easier by selecting the music that our faithful worship minister has already selected for us.)

Below are some recommendations for a biblical passage and worship songs to jump start your thinking. Notice that we have included a wide variety of styles of worship songs and hymns (all of which you can find the track to sing along with).

Exodus 20 – The Ten Commandments	*The Perfect 10* by Kathie Hill
Psalm 23 – The Lord Is My Shepherd	*The New 23rd* by Ralph Carmichael
Psalm 46 – God as our Refuge	*God Is Our Refuge* by Steve Kaban
Isaiah 40 – The Glory of the Lord	*Handel's Messiah* by George Frideric Handel
Isaiah 53 – Jesus as Suffering Servant	*Christ the Sure & Steady Anchor* by Matt Papa
Matthew 28 – Resurrection	*Christ the Lord Is Risen Today* by Charles Wesley
Luke 2 – Angels and the Shepherds	*The First Noel* (Traditional)

Hebrews 6:18-19 – God as Anchor	*Christ the Solid Rock* by Edward Mote
Revelation 1:5 – Jesus' Blood	*Are You Washed in the Blood* by Elisha A. Hoffman
Revelation 5 – Jesus as the Lion of Judah	*The Lion & the Lamb* by Big Daddy Weave

Here are a few more songs with a brief description[4]:

His Mercy Is More by Matt Boswell & Matt Papa—verses speak clearly of the gospel and God's merciful character.

Christ Our Hope in Life and Death by Keith Getty, Matt Boswell, Jordan Kauflin, Matt Merker & Matt Papa—deeply confessional modern hymn that speaks to the foundation and grounding of our faith and hope as Christians.

How Deep the Father's Love for Us by Stuart Townend—conveys the love of God in a compelling way and has a singable melody for kids.

He Will Hold Me Fast by Ada Habershon & Matt Merker—communicates the assurance of salvation clearly, while also being reliable. The idea of "being held" can resonate well with kids.

Let the Nations be Glad by Aaron Boswell, Matt Boswell & Matt Papa—strong message of God's love for the nations and his heart for missions.

Lord, I Need You by Christy Nockels, Daniel Carson, Jesse Reeves, Kristian Stanfill & Matt Maher—talks of our full dependence on Jesus, with a singable melody.

Holy, Holy, Holy by John Bacchus Dykes & Reginald Heber—gives a great overview of many of the attributes of God.

Great Is Thy Faithfulness by Thomas Obediah Chisholm & William Marion Runyan—theme of God's faithfulness that teaches the unchanging nature of God, and His unwavering love and compassion for us.

The Doxology by Louis Bourgeois & Thomas Ken—a simple song for kids that teaches huge theological implications. God is the giver of all good things, all creation should praise Him, and He is three in one.

Even though it can be uncomfortable, teach your children to praise the Lord and make a joyful noise through singing. Worship songs, hymns, and songbooks can provide meaningful direction for the family as you sing together. Sing doctrinally sound songs that are God glorifying and intentional.

My daughter and I used to sing along with a CD of my favorite Oldies from my childhood. The Four Tops, Marvin Gaye, The Spinners, Aretha Franklin, well, you know the collection. My daughter had such a good memory, excellent pitch, and sense of rhythm that she could turn the volume down to zero and keep singing the song. When she turned it back to normal volume, she would be at the exact spot in the song that the recording was, and she was on pitch and rhythm. I'm convinced your kids can do the same thing. Don't we want those skills to be in tune with God's heart and His Word?

Occasionally I'll get a Chris Tomlin or Matt Boswell praise song stuck in my head. I imagine you do the same thing. The authors of this book long for you and your family to have worship songs from your family's time together "stuck in their heads." If it sticks in their heads, then by God's grace, perhaps too it can stick in their hearts.

Endnotes

[1] Coleman, *Antiquities of the Christian Church*, 375.

[2] Alexander, *Thoughts on Family Worship*, 314.

[3] Ibid., 315.

[4] The list was first printed in the *First Irving Family Worship Guide,* by Blair Robinson. The songs were selected by the First Irving worship pastor, Kurt Bost, based on their theological soundness and familiarity to families.

CHAPTER 7

Equipping Fathers
for Teaching the Bible

After equipping fathers to study God's Word for personal worship, this chapter will provide practical ways for fathers to teach and train children in the home in the Scriptures. We provide education concepts that simplify the process for training fathers to lead and teach their children. This chapter is written for pastors to read and learn the educational concepts, and then sensibly convey them to the fathers they are equipping.

Let's say you are convinced that the two passages of Scripture introduced in previous chapters, Deuteronomy 6:4-9 and Ephesians 6:1-4 (and others), do speak directly of the responsibilities we have to our children and you want to be faithful in this role. To the lay person reading this book, we want you to grow in these practices provided. Trust that God and His Word are enough for our spiritual nourishment and growth in these areas. This is true for each of us, and we can rest in God's faithfulness.

To the pastors reading this book, we propose a different challenge. Have you thought through how you are going to train the men in your congregation? Remember, we have a responsibility as pastors to "equip the saints for the work of ministry" (Ephesians 4:12). How do we as their pastors further equip them to be faithful? How do we help them practically with obedience to the commands disclosed in God's Word?

We want to equip our men for a healthy prayer life and basic herme-neutical practices for their own spiritual good as we have discussed. And pastors can also utilize some helpful educational tools to help equip men to become teachers in their homes. The command in Deuteronomy 6 is for all fathers. This is the role of a father at home, even if he isn't gifted to teach in the church or as a profession. Pastors are to encourage all fathers to embrace their roles and faithfully teach the Scriptures to the next generation.

Teaching the Scriptures

After our own personal study and worship of God, we want to pass along God's Word to our children. We of course want to be faithful in what we teach, but we also want to be helpful. Thus, we must be consid-erate of our children, on top of being prudent. The Scriptures are living and active (Hebrews 4:12) and they are breathed out by God and are "profitable for teaching, for reproof, for correction, and for training in righteousness" (2 Timothy 3:16). We hope the Scriptures remain "liv-ing and active" in our children's lives. We cannot advocate enough that your soul is of first importance in your discipleship. To prepare for the endeavor to teach children, Alexander encourages a father to privately pre-read the passage of Scripture he will lead his family through, giving great attention to the Word of God for both himself and his family.[1]

Since knowing God is the primary responsibility of the father or mother, then teaching children about God is the second responsibility. Reading the text prior to teaching the text presents a wonderful oppor-tunity for the father to study and worship God, as well as provides an opportunity to prepare his thoughts on what he will teach his children. However, if the father is not yet mature enough in his own faith to be diligent and explanatory at this level, simply reading the Scriptures dai-ly to the family remains a necessity, as the *Directory of Family Worship* urges.[2] Opening God's Word and emphasizing its authority and truth is the basic work of fathers, with understanding that over time any father can grow in his ability to lead. Beginning this practice might be uncomfortable, but like all things, we grow in our ability to lead, explain, and teach by God's grace.

Certainly, the age of the children in the home will determine how parents' guide them through the Scriptures. For example, Whitney suggests for younger children using narrative passages and shorter sections of Scripture.[3] A helpful resource for guiding and teaching the Scriptures to children of different ages is Jason Helopoulos' book *Neglected Grace*.[4] This book delivers a healthy view of the importance of the Scriptures by also considering the various ages and levels of biblical understanding. We do not want to give children food they are not ready to eat, that could be like putting a rock on an ant! Yet we also want to teach and push them to learn and grow. The balance is tricky, which means we want to be sure we are relying on the Spirit of God on ourselves.

A few things to consider when determining how to engage with your children in the Scriptures:

- Discuss with your spouse their age level and cognitive stage. Thinking through where they are and what they understand. This will help you as you form questions to ask and the information to pass along.

- Do not assume. Do not assume they already know certain things and do not assume they are understanding what you are teaching them. Asking questions after you have taught them something will give you feedback on what they are learning and how they are learning it.

- Give them time to articulate back what you have taught. You want to see if they know certain things or how they are hearing/ learning your instruction.

- *Follow up with questions (after their responses). What does that teach you about God? How does this truth help your faith? etc.*

As a reminder, Deuteronomy 6, teaching "these words" to children in verse 7 indicates the necessity to repeat the instruction of the Lord consistently. As aforementioned in chapter 1, Turner and Coley distinguish the typical use of the Hebrew root, *shinan*, "to teach" or "repeat," from the rendering of the word in verse 7 as "a special kind of repetition—that which whets or sharpens."[5] Parents should instruct "these words" to their children by inscribing them with precision and truth onto their children's hearts. Repetitious consistency of daily discussion of the Scriptures, appears in Deuteronomy 6, to be a lifestyle that the parent must be devoted to.

The application of these imperatives should not be overcomplicated, however. We simply want to read the Bible, speak accurately about it, and simplify it enough for our children to understand. Teach and repeat. Teach and repeat. Just as Israel had responsibility for transferring the words of God to their children repeatedly and precisely, we as followers of Christ are called to do the same. A helpful tool for memorizing and teaching can be catechisms. Even if you do not come from a Christian tradition that catechized, there truly is no need to be fearful of it. *Catechism* simply means to teach or instruct. Most catechisms have a question and provide an answer with Scripture references. The point, to understand the truths about God by using Scripture. Fathers, this can be very helpful for you because they are meant to assist with the memorization of biblical truths given succinctly and accurately, nurturing children toward the ability to recall the truth learned from an early age, even if faith has not yet been given by God.

How do our brains process information?

Turner and Coley, in reference to the demands to "impress" or "teach diligently" in Deuteronomy 6:7, describe this repetitive process of learning as "connecting to *schema*" which they consider "a 21st century expression." *Schema*, simply noted, is the prior understanding and knowledge that an individual brings to a new learning episode.[6] We have identified several educational learning concepts, similar to one another, that can serve as specific tools to assist pastors with training fathers to teach for family worship, and fathers to begin implementing immediately at your kitchen tables. Coley considers *metacognition* and *reflection* practices helpful for discipling and instrumental in making teachers, fathers in this case, more effective.

What is *metacognition?* Ken Bain (2004) explains that the best college teachers discuss with their classes how to be mindful of their own mental approach to grasping and remembering new material.[7] Research reveals that greater learning takes place when a teacher shares with his class how he went about learning the material the first time he attempted it. And even greater learning occurs when students begin to share with each other how they approach learning the concepts. In this book, the aim for fathers is to help guide their children to "consciously recognize" how they best engage the thinking strategies of how they learn.[8] The process of metacognition, however, first begins with [fathers] recognizing how they, themselves, learn new material and their own mental process of learning.[9] Coley asks a helpful question to teachers:

- Have you paused in your lesson preparation to consider how you went about learning the concepts you are preparing to teach?[10]

Thinking about how one arrived at learning a new concept can help the fathers to consider how their children might learn new information. Coley suggests that fathers should describe aloud their own thinking process of how they learned what they are teaching in effort to help the children arrive at their own process of learning.[11] Tactics inside of the metacognition learning strategy can serve useful both to fathers as they teach themselves the Word, as well as how they teach their children. This process of thinking through how you (Dad) learned what you know, will help to:

- strengthen memory.
- identifying the most important points of passages.
- clarify your thoughts (by writing down what you've learned).[12]

Reflection, or reflective practice, is another helpful tool. What is *reflection*? It's simply the teacher's own evaluation of his or her effectiveness as a teacher. This practice includes evaluating and making adjustments as actions from the learners are considered, discussing best practices with other fathers, and thinking through the discipline of teaching and things to consider the next time one teaches.[13] This type of evaluation has the learner's development in mind, as well as keeps the father from repeating teaching mistakes. In addition, however, to reflecting on their own instruction, implementing reflective practice can also help fathers to consider their own heart condition before the Lord before they teach, which aligns with Moses' command to first have "these things" on their hearts.[14]

Another helpful concept is *Active Learning Techniques* (ALTs), which fathers can implement to help their children know the things of God and consider why He is to be praised. Recommended ALTs include encouraging a child to think back on particular seasons or moments in life that are related to the teaching moment, having a child read and interact with the Scripture if they are of age and ability, and having them write certain things down meant to spur on greater reflection and assessment.[15] These practices can help build deeper understanding within the child. In creating a culture where children actively think about the glorious deeds of God, the heart of worship and response can be cultivated. Introducing basic engagement activities that fathers can implement will also be helpful in preparing fathers to lead in family worship. With worldly inundation occurring in many Christian homes, the pervasive description of the all-encompassing worship of God commanded forth in this text ought to encourage and inspire the Christian home to become inundated with the worship of God. Family worship provides an opportunity for families to read, discuss, and implement "these words," the covenant commands of God to His people.

In the title of her article, "Road Tested / Chunk-Challenge-Chew-Chat-Check," author Emily Mather presents a simple but powerful outline for fathers to use as they develop a child-friendly approach to teaching Scripture. Step one, a parent slices the passage into separate pieces. Of course, the size depends on the age and spiritual development of the children. Next, the parent then presents questions or tasks that challenge the child to think more deeply about the truth in the passage. Third, for a brief period (30 seconds up to several minutes) the child can process the new information. Fourth, conversation can take place that gives the child the opportunity to put things in his/her own words. And finally, in addition to the last two steps, the parents can assess their children's level of understanding.[16] There are five phases in this model of instruction that can be adapted to teaching and learning Scripture as a family.

Chunk: Parent communicates new content into slices lasting no more than ten minutes.

Challenge: Parent presents a targeted question or task that guides the children to delve deeper into the content.

Chew: Parent provides children an allotted amount of time to process information and engage their minds by reflecting or writing out their understanding of the content.

Chat: Children are provided the opportunity to express their emerging understanding, and provides an opportunity for the parent to assess, probe, and engage the children to further help their understanding.

Check: Parent gives a final targeted check for understanding by allowing students to briefly respond to a targeted question.[17] With Paul's emphasis on the "instruction and discipline of the Lord" (Ephesians 6:4) to be given by fathers, this simple lesson outline is a user-friendly and effective approach for education.

Scripture Memorization

A simple exercise to further implement each of these practices and to further know and remember God's Word is through Scripture memorization. Simply take a passage you and your family are working through and begin to memorize chunks of it at a time. We encourage you to not move on from memorizing a passage until each family member can confidently recite it. Even the process of misremembering, or stumbling through a text, can ultimately be helpful as the passage becomes more and more familiar to the child (and parent). You can practice speaking the passage when you are in family worship at the table, or when you are driving in your car, or when walking a trail by your house. And just as you apply questions to your Bible teaching time, apply those same questions during your memorization segments.

Most recently, my family (Blair) has been learning 2 Timothy 3:16-17: "All Scripture is breathed out by God and profitable for teaching, for reproof, for correction, and for training in righteousness, that the man of God may be complete, equipped for every good work." We have been studying the text and then taking sections of it at a time and memorizing it (I have two boys, ages nine and six, so we have taken our time through this particular passage). What my wife and I were not expecting is that our little girl (who is three) recited half the passage by memory the other day after each of us were saying it to one another. Unbeknownst to us, she had been listening the whole time we've been speaking it to one another. Scripture memorization and consideration is a wonderful tool for the family.

Encouragement for Pastors

Pastors, for you specifically, these educational concepts and practices can encourage the men in your congregation to begin implementing simple instruction of the Scriptures with their children. These concepts are easy to consider, easy to teach, and easy to apply to your ministry as you seek to equip fathers. After training fathers in basic hermeneutics and prayer, we propose training sessions in which you can walk through these educational concepts with the fathers of your congregation. The concept structures and examples in the back of the book are meant to serve as a guide for you in your equipping and in the father's learning.

Ultimately, faith comes by hearing the words of Christ (Romans 10:17) and we know that God is the giver of faith so no one may boast (Ephesians 2:8-9). This is a work of the Spirit of God. Thus, we provide opportunities for the Word to be heard and memorized that it may take root in our children, and as fathers, we rest in God's work knowing that salvation belongs to Him. As pastors, we help the fathers of our congregations understand this glorious work God is willing to do.

Here Is a Breakdown of What We Just Covered

Metacognition: fathers recognize how they, themselves, learn new material and their own mental process of learning.

- Have you paused in your lesson preparation to consider how you went about learning the concepts you are preparing to teach?
- Based on how you learned the concept, think back through how you learned something and then describe that process to your children.

Reflecting with children on a particular point of the text

- Interaction with Scripture (if they can, have them read and reflect)
- Writing or drawing exercises to enhance reflection and assessment
- Scripture memorization

Family Worship Inside a Teaching/Learning Structure (The 5 Cs)

- *Chunk: ten-minute intervals*
- *Challenge: a targeted question*
- *Chew: allotted amount of time for learner to consider*
- *Chat: learner is provided opportunity to express understanding*
- *Check: teacher gives a final targeted question for understanding and allows learned to respond (summary of main point)*

Endnotes

[1] Alexander, *Thoughts on Family Worship*, 311.

[2] *The Directory of Family Worship*, Section III.

[3] Whitney, *Family Worship*, 44-45.

[4] Helopoulos, Jason. *A Neglected Grace: Family Worship in the Christian Home* (Ross-shire, Scotland: Christian Focus, 2013), 53.

[5] Coley and Turner, "Examining Deuteronomy 6," 10.

[6] Ken Coley, *Teaching for Change: Eight Keys for Transformational Bible Study with Teens* (Nashville, TN: Randall House, 2017), 50.

[7] Ken Bain, *What the Best College Teachers Do* (Cambridge, MA: Harvard Press, 2004), 25.

[8] Ibid.

[9] Coley, *Teaching for Change*, 50-51.

[10] Ibid., 51.

[11] Ibid., 54.

[12] Ibid., 54-55.

[13] Ibid., 56-58.

[14] Coley and Turner, "Examining Deuteronomy 6," 8.

[15] Coley, *Teaching for Change*, 29-31.

[16] Emily Mather, "Chunk-Challenge-Chew-Chat-Check," *EU 57* (2015): 7, http://www.ascd.org/publications/newsletters/education_update/jun15/vol57/num06/Chunk-Challenge-Chew-Chat-Check.aspx.

[17] Ibid., 7.

PART 3

POINT TO THE ANCIENT PATHS

Chapter 8

Training Proposals and Structures for Training Fathers

Chapter eight discusses different training structures and options for pastors in training the fathers in the congregation. The chapter will examine what to cover during training sessions with fathers, the length and time-extent of training sessions, practical ways to implement the hermeneutics, prayer, worship, and educational concepts in these training sessions, and general leadership suggestions when equipping fathers that the authors have discovered through experience.[1]

Very simply put, fathers in local churches need to be encouraged and equipped. Encouragement should always happen, and oftentimes, encouragement and equipping should go together. In this chapter, we will lay out some simple categories and suggestions for equipping, which we recognize these recommendations are not all encompassing; hoping they can easily be added-to, scaled down, or modified to fit better into another context. Some of these ideas have been implemented in local churches and they are successful. Again, these are not exhaustive models, but simple structures and categories for the purpose of being adaptable to whatever fits your ministry convictions or church context.

For the purpose of being clear and concise, we break down our equipping aims into two basic concepts: *1) Responsibilities fathers have to lead in family worship*, and *2) Fathers lead their families as an extension of the local church.* These two concepts are then the focus of living workshops for men to be educated and encouraged, to practice and discuss these concepts, and then to hold each other accountable to what God has ordained while building a culture within the local body that is breeding fathers who are faithfully walking out their responsibilities to their families. These living workshops can also be called equipping classes or sessions. We believe these two concepts are a great place to start your equipping.

Concept 1: Responsibilities Fathers Have to Lead in Family Worship

Inside the first concept are two major concentrations. The first concentration is to prepare fathers in their own personal worship. A heart surrendered unto the Lord is of primary importance, so that a father can then lead and disciple his family. The applications for this are training fathers with a basic hermeneutic skill set and teaching them to pray and rely on the Holy Spirit. The second concentration in the first concept is training fathers how to lead in family worship; specifically, how to teach and repeat God's Word to their children, how to worship with their families, and how to represent Christ in the home. The applications for this concentration are equipping fathers with basic educational learning concepts and creating space in the home for God to be praised; more particularly, singing praise songs in the family and praying in the family.

Concept 2: Fathers Lead the Families as an Extension of the Local Church (little church)

Inside the second concept are two major concentrations: The first concentration is to have fathers implement a read, pray, and sing family worship structure in their families. And the second concentration is to develop a MASTER Plan for accountability and checkpoints, mobilization, and continuing education—all for the sake of the health of the local church. The second concept focuses on the unity and accountability of the families with the local church, and the first concept focuses on individual fathers' responsibilities with their families. Timothy Paul Jones and John David Trentham, in their book entitled *Practical Family Ministry*, introduce a master plan for equipping parents to disciple their children, a plan known by the acronym MASTER.[2] MASTER stands for *Model* what you want parents to do, *Articulate* expected changes with key leaders, *Schedule* key checkpoints, *Train* every teacher to be a parent equipper, *Empathize* with parents who are struggling, *Recruit* families to share testimonies. We have taken certain aspects of Jones and Trentham's model and find them very useful for equipping. Specifically, we have identified the following components of their model and modified them for our purposes: (1) develop a specific list of practices that will help fathers disciple their children, (2) implement checkpoints in the plan that evaluate the progress of fathers, (3) provide continued equipping for fathers, (4) mobilize fathers leading in family worship to provide help and encouragement to fathers who are not, and (5) motivate fathers with testimonies that speak to the hardships and blessings of family worship.[3]

To keep it simple, we have broken down the training of these two concepts into four living workshops. This model suggests meeting once a week for four weeks. However, you could have eight sessions for training instead of four, or you could train men one Sunday night a month for one year. Whatever and whenever you choose to do it really does not matter as much as holding fast to equipping fathers in the concepts and principles God has laid out for us to implement.

First Meeting (Introduction to Family Worship)

During the first equipping meeting, it is helpful to build out the argument for the importance of family worship and discipleship. For example, walking through Scriptures that speak directly to this responsibility is the firm place we stand. Scriptures like: Deuteronomy 6:4-9; Psalm 78:1-8; and Ephesians 6:1-4 are an easy place to start. Showing the fathers what the Scriptures convey about the role of fathers is foundational for this equipping model.

We have also found it helpful to provide a historical overview, like sampled in chapter 2, that builds the argument out further. Learning how men from the past have led their families is a great motivator. We recommend focusing chiefly on the elements of family worship: *read, pray,* and *sing.* This may help the men feel less intimidated when they see how simple family worship can be. Reviewing practices in church history can also help to build conviction, commitment, and culture, especially if the men work through some of the great resources from the past. You may find it helpful to share Richard Baxter's ten motivations (why fathers should lead in family worship), Oliver Heywood's ten practical suggestions (how fathers can lead in family worship), and J. W. Alexander's nine objections (why fathers do not lead in family worship).

Along the same lines, there are several great modern resources that can be helpful to introduce these basic concepts during this first meeting as well. To name a few: Joel Beeke's *How Should Men Lead Their Families,* Donald Whitney's *Family Worship, Neglected Grace: Family Worship in the Christian Home* by Jason Helopoulos, and *Gospel Family: Cultivating Family Discipleship, Family Worship, & Family Missions* by Jonathan Williams. Each of these resources, and others like them, offer unique, but similar thoughts on family worship. Choose elements that you believe are most beneficial and equip from there.

After the time of family worship introduction, argument, and conviction building, the first meeting should end with a time of prayer and praise amongst the men present at the workshop. As the fathers leave the first meeting, they have assignments to complete before the second meeting (the next week or so). For example, assignments could be:

- Have men read Joel Beeke's *How Should Men Lead Their Families*
- Have the men discuss the material learned during first meeting with their spouses[4]

Second Meeting (Concept 1—Equipping)

To begin the second meeting, fathers should be given an opportunity to deliberate about family worship during roundtable discussion. The fathers can discuss the book they were assigned to read; in this case, they will discuss and review Joel Beeke's, *How Should Men Lead Their Families*, and then corporately discuss some of the observations from the book led by a leader or pastor. This is also the time that the fathers can discuss the conversations they had with their spouses throughout the week. The intent is to cultivate a culture of encouragement, expectation, and shared lives through these conversations.

The primary goal for the second meeting is equipping fathers for personal worship. Fathers should be trained in a basic hermeneutic, which will help them learn to determine the meaning of the biblical texts. Even if men know how to study God's Word, simply helping them connect their study to their fatherly responsibility is needed for many. There are several methods for training that you can use, and typically each of us have preferences in our hermeneutical methods. Please use the example questions in chapter 4 if you find them helpful. Another popular method is the *Inductive Bible Study Method* (Observations, Explanation/Interpretation, Applications). We also think one of the most helpful hermeneutical paradigms is found in Nick Roark and Robert Cline's book *Biblical Theology*. They use five interpretative lenses for examining the biblical text, and they have made it simple by having each lens begin with the letter C: *Context, Covenant, Canon, Character of God,* and *Christ*.[5]

Moving forward in the workshop, lead fathers through hermeneutical exercises, and then provide both opportunity for roundtable conversations and corporate conversations. Give them a passage to consider and work through, and then discuss. This builds confidence and habits.

Now, we know that man cannot grow apart from the work of God. This is also a good meeting to begin discussing with the fathers about the practice of prayer in their personal lives. Introduce prayer paradigms and provide prayer categories for the fathers, as well as encouragement to be faithful in the discipline and dependent on the Spirit.[6]

In closing the second meeting, fathers will once again spend time in prayer and in worship. Fathers are assigned the same three passages of Scripture to practice the hermeneutics taught during the meeting. Fathers journal their personal worship experience and compile notes from their hermeneutics practice. The fathers are to come prepared to the third meeting to share during roundtable and corporate discussions (if the group is large enough). Fathers are instructed to spend specific time praying for themselves and their families. And finally, fathers will continue to observe their family's habits and rhythms; seeking to establish a consistent time to meet with them for family worship as is agreed upon by their spouses.

Third Meeting (Concept 1—Equipping)

To begin the third meeting, fathers will discuss at their roundtables what they discovered in their time of biblical study, prayer, and personal worship. Again, building a culture of encouragement, expectation, accountability, and practice is critical for the fathers in a local church. At their tables, it would be good to discuss the observations of their family's schedule and when the family could possibly gather for family worship throughout the week. This conversation is intended to have fathers encourage one another to find the time and fight for the time. The need for families to gather around the table and under the authority of

Scripture is a priority, and leaders should continue to keep this priority in front of the men they train.

The primary goal of the third meeting is for fathers to build upon their personal hermeneutic skill sets by learning how to teach their children the Scriptures. Several helpful learning and teaching concepts were previously discussed: *Metacognition, Reflection, Active Learning Techniques* (ALTs), and a simple lesson outline for fathers to give instruction called the 5 C's (*chunk, challenge, chew, chat, check*).[7] These concepts practically go along with the basic questions provided to fathers for asking different aged children questions from Scripture.

One does not need to be a trained educator to learn these concepts. They are basic, simple, explanatory, and helpful. Merely introducing these ideas can create firm ground for fathers to stand on when thinking about implementing teaching. These concepts provide fathers with a plan on how to engage their families. Each father will implement according to his personality and make up, but these concepts serve as a "staircase" in helping fathers reach new floors of interaction, precision, and shepherding.

In addition to teaching, we also want to keep before the men simple prayer points and singing suggestions as already outlined in this book. Ask your music minister to provide some resources like a list of the top 20 popular songs used in your church's worship services or a playlist on YouTube, Spotify, or your church website. Review those resources with the fathers and encourage them to begin implementing basic measures of each within their family structures. Remember, you are crafting for most of them a new vision for their home. Encouragement, and focus on God's worth and glory, should always accompany the instruction.

End the third meeting with prayer and praise time for the fathers. This will create worship and response in the hearts of our men as they consider their role in leading family worship. Before attending the fourth and final meeting, encourage the men to begin implementing these basic practices in family worship along with continuing to implement personal worship practices—Scripture study and prayer. In continuing to press each personal and family worship principle, have fathers journal their experience in family worship and come prepared at the fourth meeting to share with other fathers of their experiences. One final idea that I received from my friend, Jonathan Williams, is to have fathers begin putting together a family mission statement. This statement is meant to hone their focus on their family responsibility and mission even more.

Fourth Meeting (Concept 2—Equipping)
(Include wives and kids above sixth grade)

The fourth and final meeting will include the wives of the fathers who have been in training the three weeks prior, as well as children in the sixth grade and above to introduce the topic of family worship by someone other than their father who can simultaneously learn what is expected of their father. This also gives pastors and leaders an opportunity to continue building out the larger footprint of expectation and culture within a local body; especially addressing wives and children with regard to God's expectations in the home and how they can promote that culture in the home.

After the first three meetings focused on building conviction, commitment, culture, and skill sets, which focus on Concept 1, this final meeting will focus on Concept 2 and introduce actual models of family worship for practice in the home.[8] Have yourself, or a volunteer or two, demonstrate the practicality of family worship taught from a table at the front of the room, which is set up like a normal dinner table.[9] Demonstrating what this can look like can burn off fears for other men. Another way to capture demonstration is to have fathers video their family worship time the week prior and then play a handful of those videos to show as examples. Each will be unique and different; each will encourage.

During this meeting as well, you can also introduce the idea of catechisms. Some of your fathers will come from backgrounds where they are not familiar with catechisms or have certain connotations of what catechisms are. Addressing questions such as *"what is a catechism?"; "how do I use a catechism?"; "why are they important?"*; and *"what catechism(s) should I use?"* Simply put, catechisms are a helpful method to learn the Scriptures and develop theological categories. Though the term catechism may be equated with another denomination or church branch, there is a rich history of catechism practice within most of the major denominations. It is simply a tool used to train children and new believers (adults too) in the faith. The Greek word for "instruct/train" or "teach" is *katecheo*, and from this word comes the English word for catechize (and ultimately catechism). *Katecheo* is used in passages such as Romans 2:18, 1 Corinthians 14:19, Galatians 6:6, and four other places in the New Testament. Here are two catechisms we recommend (though there are many more):

- *Spurgeon's Catechism: With Scriptural Proofs* by Charles Spurgeon
- *The New City Catechism: 52 Questions & Answers for Our Hearts & Minds* by Tim Keller

And finally, during this meeting, fathers will share their mission statements (or completed parts of their mission statements) with their roundtables. This encourages fathers to be intentional with the role that God has ordained each of them to commit to. Unveiling these mission statements together strengthens the culture and expectations, immediately.

After the Primary Equipping Stages

A significant part in fulfilling Concept 2 is ensuring that a healthy culture of accountability prevails after the living workshops. Family worship is a family duty, as well as a congregational responsibility. The MASTER Plan for the health of the families in the church is discussed during this meeting (or perhaps in another meeting separately). The MASTER Plan focuses on three specific areas: checkpoints and accountability, mobilization, and continuing education. Addressing each of these areas, the fathers will gather a few times a year for the purpose of sharing testimonies and for continuing education/equipping. It might be good to handout a few basic accountability questions at these follow-up meetings to evaluate how the fathers are leading in family worship.

Pastors and leaders, we encourage you to mobilize fathers who are faithfully leading their families in family worship in hopes of encouraging fathers who are not. Mobilizing fathers can be accomplished in one-on-one meetings, or by having families into one another's home to practice family worship together. In addition, offer the same equipping workshops a couple of times a year so fathers who have not gone through the training, and new members who have recently joined, can attend and be equipped. Important too, is encouraging fathers to utilize the discipleship structures already in place in your local church to bring about advocacy, accountability, and community with fathers/men. If these forums already have accountability as a part of the cultures, adding the responsibility to lead in family worship to the groups' cultures should be natural.

Here Is a Simple Outline of a Living Workshop:

CONCEPT 1: *Responsibilities fathers have to lead in family worship*
- Personal Worship: Know God's Word

  Equip fathers with basic hermeneutic and prayer paradigms for fathers
- Family Worship: Teach and repeat God's Word to children (instruct and worship, and represent Christ)
  Equip fathers with basic educational learning concepts
  - Create space for God to be praised for His "glorious deeds"
    - Singing praise songs in the family (see list in *Family Worship Guide*)

- Pray with our families (and teach them to pray)

CONCEPT 2: *Fathers lead the families as an extension of the local church ("little church")*

- Leading in Read, Pray, Sing (encourage a simple structure of family worship in the home– practiced throughout the church; consider the structures provided)
- MASTER Plan: for checkpoints/oversight, accountability, mobilization, and continuing education (all for the sake of the health of the church)

Here Is an Outline of the Four Living Workshops (as an example):

First Meeting (Introduction to Family Worship)

Building the Argument:

- Scriptural instruction
  - ° Deuteronomy 6:4-9
  - ° Psalm 78:1-8
  - ° Ephesians 6:1-4
- Historical review
  - ° Read, Pray, Sing elements identified

Building Our Convictions, Commitments, and Culture:

- *Baxter's ten motivations* (why fathers should lead in family worship)
- *Heywood's ten practical suggestions* (how fathers can lead in family worship)
- *Alexander's nine objections* (why fathers don't lead in family worship)

- *Beeke's paradigm*: prophet, priest, king (three offices fathers are called to in family worship)

Worship: (the fathers/men pray and worship together)

Assignments Before the Next Class:

- Read Beeke's: How Should Men Lead Their Families?
- Review material discussed
- Discuss family worship with your spouse
  - ° Husbands asks spouses to help evaluate/observe family's weekly schedule; helping determine where family worship could fit in consistently within the rhythms of the home
  - ° Husbands ask wives to (hold them/encourage them in) the biblical role of father as discussed

Second Meeting (Concept 1—Equipping)

Round Table:

- Review Beeke's book (collect thoughts from fathers)
- Discuss conversations with spouses
- Personal testimony to be shared for encouragement (selected by pastors)

Equipping for Personal Worship:

- Hermeneutics (equipping):
  - ° God-centered Hermeneutics
  - ° Inductive Bible Study Method (Observations, Explanation/ Interpretation, Applications)
  - ° Five Cs of Interpretation (Context, Covenant, Canon, Character of God, Christ)
  - ° Scripture Memorization discussion
- Prayer (discuss)
  - ° Discuss prayer topics and paradigms

Worship: (the fathers/men pray and worship together)

Assignments Before Next Meeting:

- Begin implementing these practices into personal study
  - ○ Same three verses are given to all fathers to begin practicing biblical hermeneutics (fathers are to study the verses before the next meeting)
    - Fathers journal their personal worship experience and compile notes from hermeneutic practice (come prepared at the third meeting to share during table discussions)
    - (Option: provide fathers with Terry L. Johnson's Bible Reading Plan)
- Spend specific time praying for yourself and your family
- Continue to observe your family's habits and rhythms; seeking to establish a consistent time to meet with them

Third Meeting (Concept 1—Equipping)

Round Table (equipping review):

- Fathers discuss what they discovered in their time of biblical study
- Fathers discuss with one another their personal (and family) worship experiences since last meeting
- Discuss the observations of the family's schedule and when the family could possibly gather
- Personal testimony to be shared for encouragement (selected by pastors)

Equipping for Family Worship:

- Train in Educational Concepts (Metacognition; Reflections; ALTs; Lesson Outline 5 Cs: Chunk, Challenge, Chew, Chat, Check)
  - ○ Get to questions like: What is the main meaning of the text?

- Navigating the different ages (using children's pastor and student pastor to teach), explaining in simple terms
- Scripture Memorization discussion
- Prayer (discuss)
  - Discuss prayer topics (provided in this project)
- Singing praise songs (discuss)
  - The practice of worshiping through song as a family

Worship: (the fathers/men pray and worship together)

Assignments:

- Begin implementing these practices in family worship. Walk through with fathers that need to repent to family or who have never done this. Possibly provide a testimony to encourage.
- Continuing implementing personal worship practices (hermeneutics and prayer).
- Fathers journal their experience in family worship and come prepared at the third meeting to share with other fathers of their experience.
- Begin putting together a family mission statement.

Fourth Meeting (Concept 2—Equipping)
(Wives are included and kids above 6th grade)

Couples Round Table:

- Fathers discuss with one another their personal and family worship experiences since last meeting

The Practical Structures and Guides for Family Worship:

- Models to consider
- Actual demonstration of family worship ("teaching from a table")

- Catechisms (what is a catechism?; how do I use them?; why is it important?; Suggested catechisms)

Family Mission Statement:

- Mission statement for the home (final)
  - Fathers are to share their mission statement with their families and those they walk with in community

Thinking Past the Workshops

MASTER Plan (the health of the whole church):

- Guarding our responsibilities:

  Checkpoints/accountability, mobilization, and continuing education
  - Every three months: gather fathers for prayer, testimony, and continuing education
  - Survey/evaluate how the men are leading in family worship (a few basic accountability questions each time)
  - Mobilize those who are practicing family worship to bring people into their homes to model family worship
- Offer four-week Living Workshop (twice a year; any father/man can attend)
- Use structures already in place (Community Groups, Sunday School, D-Groups, etc.) to bring advocacy, accountability, and community to fathers/men
  - Encourage fathers to connect with men in these settings to help them walk faithfully in their responsibilities (a charge to each father)
- Discuss with wives how men are to be encouraged and held accountable in the home
  Worship (the fathers/men/wives pray and worship together)
  - Implement an annual Family Worship weekend at a campground

This *Living Workshop* is merely an idea for equipping fathers in a local congregation. It can be adapted a thousand different ways. We simply want you to see what equipping could look like and some direction for you to begin the process.

Endnotes

[1] The training concepts for this chapter were formed through a strategy model made up of fathers from First Baptist Church Irving, Texas who served a crucial role in Blair Robinson's dissertation project and partnered with him in ministry.

[2] Timothy Paul Jones and John David Trentham, *Practical Family Ministry: A Collection of Ideas for Your Church* (Nashville, TN: Randall House, 2015), 75-76.

[3] Ibid.

[4] Husbands are to ask their spouse to help evaluate and observe the family's weekly schedule; helping determine where family worship could fit in consistently within the rhythms of the home. As well, husbands are to ask their wives to hold them accountable and encourage them in the biblical role of father as discussed.

[5] Nick Roark and Robert Cline, *Biblical Theology: How the Church Faithfully Teaches the Gospel* (Wheaton, IL: Crossway, 2018), 88-99. Each of the five lenses are defined and very helpful for teaching people to rightly study God's Word. We encourage those looking for a resource to consult chapter 5 of Roark and Cline's *Biblical Theology*.

[6] Refer here to previously provided prayer paradigms.

[7] See Appendix C, page 114-115 for basic descriptions of each educational learning concept and strategy.

[8] Resources for family worship models can be found in [Appendix A].

[9] Jonathan Williams, author of *Gospel Family*, practices this instruction and provided this idea during previous research.

Chapter 9

Providing Continual Oversight to Family Household Leaders

Part of establishing a culture of fathers leading their families to praise and worship God in the home is having healthy and accountable oversight occurring across church leadership. This chapter will cover how to create a healthy oversight of these practices throughout the church and how church leadership must establish the culture, practice, accountability, and pace for family worship. If the Lord has commanded these practices for fathers, church leaders must provide pastoral oversight, which faithfully encourages church members new and old to partake in God's glorious design for the family.

As believers, we should understand that it is a tremendous blessing to be a part of a local church. The Church is where the nations are collected and worship the Living God that has saved them and made them righteous through Christ Jesus. And this has been the amazing plan of God first revealed to Abraham in Genesis 12:2-3. In God's kindness, *the faith*, which is grounded in Christ Jesus and the expressed hope we have in the glorious gospel of God, was delivered once for all to the saints—*the Church* (Jude 3). And the Church, as Mark Dever puts it, *"is the collection of people who are hearing the Word of God, responding to it with their lives, and who have obeyed Jesus' specific commands to be baptized and proclaim his death in the Lord's Supper."* We are a people set apart by God to glorify Him, serve and disciple one another, and who are commanded to be intentional in reaching the lost people of the world by bringing them the gospel. God's Church is the community of God's people redeemed through Christ and regenerated by the Holy Spirit. The people who have put their faith in Christ for their salvation, repented of their sin, and are found righteous in Him.

Paul says of the Church in Ephesians 2:19-22:

> So then you are no longer strangers and aliens, but you are fellow citizens with the saints and members of the household of God, [20] built on the foundation of the apostles and prophets, Christ Jesus himself being the cornerstone, [21] in whom the whole structure, being joined together, grows into a holy temple in the Lord. [22] In him you also are being built together into a dwelling place for God by the Spirit.

We have responsibilities and joys to serve one another (1 Corinthians 10:31; Galatians 6:1-2), devote ourselves to God's Word and prayer (Acts 2:42-47), to make disciples of all nations (Matthew 28:18-20), offer our bodies as a living sacrifice to God (Romans 12:1-2), and to live in light of Christ's return (1 Peter 4:7-11). We are in the process of growing into maturity in Christ (Ephesians 4:11-13) and are being transformed into the same image (2 Corinthians 3:18). It is so glorious to be a part of the Church of the Living God.

So, what does the local church have to do with Family Worship and Family Ministry?

Everything.

Individual Christian households are never separate from the household of God and the gracious structures and polity that His Word reveals for His glory and the good of His people. God *gifts* the Church with pastors and teachers to equip the saints for the work of ministry (Ephesians 4:11-12)—men who are qualified to teach and lead (1 Timothy 3:8-13), helpful instruction for when we gather for worship (Matthew 18:17; 1 Corinthians 11-14; Ephesians 5:18-21; 1 Timothy 3:14–5:25; Titus 1:5-9; Hebrews 10:24-25). The local church is not a place someone "goes," but a people from different households that covenant together under the authority of Christ.

A Word to Pastors

1) Set the example

By God's grace and wisdom, pastor, you have been placed over a people who belong to God that you are called to lead and shepherd. You are to do this willingly, not out of compulsion, greed, or abusive authority, but eagerly serving as an example to the flock (1 Peter 5:1-3). Setting an example in life, faith, and conduct.

One of the qualifications for pastoral oversight is men who have their households in order, with all dignity, which includes children who are submissive (1 Timothy 3:4-5; Titus 1:6). Pastors, we set the tone in our local churches for how the home is to function, we are to live out expectations God has given to us, and we are to encourage other fathers to do the very same. Invite people into your home to be near you and your family as you faithfully live out your example before them. One thing my wife and I do is invite families and couples into our home and participate in family worship together. Let members of your congregation see how you lead your family so they can be encouraged to do the same. Worship is not meant to be ridged, but both reverent and flexible, and filled with joy from the Holy Spirit.

2) Equip the saints

On one hand, Scripture describes pastors as ones who equip the saints for the work of ministry (Ephesians 4:12). On the other hand, written a little later in Paul's same letter, we see that fathers are to bring up their children in the disciple and instruction of the Lord (Ephesians 6:4).

Very naturally, then, we see how these two responsibilities must both occur, and can go together. Perhaps it helps to say it this way: ***Pastors, equip fathers for the work of ministry in the home, which is to bring their children up in the discipline and instruction of the Lord.*** Equipping fathers for the work of ministry in the home is not the only equipping responsibilities pastors are called to oversee in the local church, but it should always be a part of the equipping ministry you oversee.

Many churches and ministries today offer programs or curriculums to guide people through family discipleship material. These resources can certainly be helpful in making disciples and in fulfilling paternal responsibilities and praise the Lord so many resources have been provided. Though putting curriculum in the hands of fathers can be a supportive starting place, equipping fathers for the work of ministry is different than giving fathers ministry to do. Essentially that is why we wrote this book. Equipping requires prayer and training, it includes growth and struggle, and is most helpful when the "long approach" is in view. Equipping is not simply supplying material, and then talking about it a few times. It is an intentional culture that never goes away. Be with the fathers in their journey toward faithfulness. On top of exemplifying God's order, train them. Pray with them. Walk with them. And hold them accountable to the Lord, their families, and the church.

3) Define the relationship between church and home

Pastors, we are to help define for our people how the local church and the home operate together. It is important that our people understand how the church worships together when we are gathered, what fathers are responsible for, and not responsible for, when the family is together, and why this distinction is important. There are lines of distinction, yet one body striving toward unity and seeking God's glory.

As we already mentioned, the home is to operate as a "little church." And this is true … ***in part***. Fathers carry out worship responsibilities that are also practiced in local churches, for example: Scripture study and teaching, prayer and praise, encouragement, admonishment, and shepherding. These are essential practices to the Christian faith that are not limited to a church building but extends to all areas of a covenant community and individual lives.

So yes, the home does act like a "little church" in some ways, but not in others. There are two areas in particular that need to be considered. *The first*, pastors still oversee the flock even beyond the borders of the church building. The pastor remains responsible before the Lord for the worship in the home. The father, though he acts as a pastor and priest in the home and will be held accountable before the Lord for his leadership in the home, is still under the authority of the overseers (Acts 20:28; 1 Thessalonians 5:12; 1 Peter 5:1; Hebrews 13:7). So fathers are not to go rogue in their leadership, and pastors are to empower fathers to serve and lead—yet still keep watch over their souls and the souls of their family members.

Secondly, the home is not to act separately from the church in participating in the ordinances of the church, specifically, *Baptism* and *the Lord's Supper*. Richard Baxter is helpful in distinguishing between worship in the home and worship in the congregation as he addressed the matter specifically. Baxter reserved baptism and the Lord's Supper for congregational gatherings only, and the church has historically practiced the same thing. The Scriptures describe these two ordinances as practiced amongst congregations. These two ordinances are given *to the Church* to visibly proclaim the gospel to a congregation.

Paul gives instruction in 1 Corinthians 11:17-34 for the right way to institute and practice the Lord's Supper for ... *"when you come together."* The Table is not a separate meal, but rather a corporate meal in which we worship Christ together because He has established the New Covenant in His blood, and because He is coming again ... and we proclaim His death (together!) until He returns. Baptism is the same. Baptism is a command for all disciples of Christ to obey after repentance and is the mark of believers (Matthew 28:19; Acts 2:38). We are buried with Christ in death, raised to walk in new life (Romans 6:4). Baptism is the first public declaration of a new believer and is affirmation from the congregation that the new believer's faith is real. And baptism, seen throughout the New Testament, is always affiliated with newly formed churches or established churches; never isolated from a congregation or overseer. Baptism is public knowledge as seen throughout the Gospels, Acts, and the Epistles, it is not a private practice.

Jesus gives the *keys to the kingdom* (authority) to the disciples (Matthew 16:19), and the disciples established the church, on the authority of Christ, with pastors/overseers to continue the work of making disciples. Disciples are those who have faith in Christ, have repented of sin (Mark 1:15), and have been baptized into Christ and His church; with local bodies of believers being established (Acts 6:1-7; Acts 8:26-40; Acts 16; Romans 5-8; 1 Corinthians 1; Galatians 3:26-28; Colossians 2:11-13; 1 Timothy 3:1-7; and Titus 1:5-9). Pastors, we oversee God's people. We disciple, teach, admonish, exhort, affirm, and counsel the people the Lord has asked us to steward. We lead them in the celebration of the Lord's Supper and baptism.

How do we oversee the souls of fathers?

Every local church has its own size, culture, and practices. The churches I have served are very different from one another. Which is to say, there is not one exact art or way to oversee souls. However, we are called to oversee:

> So I exhort the elders among you, as a fellow elder and a witness of the sufferings of Christ, as well as a partaker in the glory that is going to be revealed: shepherd the flock of God that is among you, exercising oversight, not under compulsion, but willingly, as God would have you; not for shameful gain, but eagerly; not domineering over those in your charge, but being examples to the flock (1 Peter 5:1-3).

Though there is not an exact paradigm to present to you that says, "You must do it this way!" There are principles of oversight and shepherding grounded in Scripture and must be implemented, bathed in prayer, and require the sacrifice as alluded to in Peter's words above. To neglect this responsibility is to neglect what God has asked pastors to fundamentally do for Him, and for His people.

We suggest a few things to implement in conjunction with some of the equipping suggestions in chapter 8:

Divide out the oversight: if you have several pastors or elders leading your congregation, divide out responsibilities of oversight, check-ins/follow ups, encouragement, and equipping responsibilities. If you are a solo pastor, the work remains the same (with encouragement to raise up advocates who can help you lead). Deacons can also help to serve in this ministry (though we do not see this as a primary function of deacon responsibility as it pertains to the ministry of the Word, which Scripture assigns to pastor/elder responsibilities).

Hold men to the standard that God does and be gracious as God is: our culture today influences men in a myriad of directions, and really seeks to minimize the responsibilities, priorities, and basic purposes of fathers. This narrative is everywhere right now. So we must go after fathers and teach them what God has for them and their families. We chase them like a shepherd does his sheep. We hold them to God's Word and we remind them of God's grace.

Inform and *Remind*: We all have really leaky brains; meaning we forget important things often. Our congregants need to be taught and informed of God's Word, but this really is only the beginning of equipping. Reminding them is hard work. Keep it in front of them in sermon applications, small group questions, weekly emails, and prayer points. Let this narrative shape your ministry to the church. There are many important pieces of ministry, and ministry to fathers is not the only responsibility you have, but it is important to establish the institution of the home, which God has designed.

Pray: all of your ministry effort is in vain apart from God working. We must pray for this work. Our staffs must pray for this work. We must teach our fathers and mothers to pray for God to work and move and have His way. This is the most important aspect to equipping fathers is appealing to God for help. He is the One who sanctifies; thus, we trust in Him. If we enter this work without trusting the Lord, we are fools.

A Word to Fathers

Hopefully, this book is a helpful resource to you. The heart behind it is to equip you to fulfill the wonderful role God has providentially granted. Though it is glorious work, it is hard work. Be dedicated to growing, learning, and practicing these things. The Great Commission is to be fulfilled, and the first place to start *for you*, is your home. We wanted to provide you with a few encouragements to keep before you as fathers, sons of God, and members of local churches:

Follow those God has placed over you (Hebrews 13:17): God has graciously placed pastors and overseers over you as you walk out this responsibility. Listen to their instruction and submit to them with joy and not groaning. Let them freely encourage and instruct you, and even admonish or rebuke should you need it. They will give an account for your soul and the members of your household. Pray for them and encourage them and apply what they teach—it is for your good.

Commit to this work: Your kids will not be in your home forever. As I type this, my oldest son Abel (who is 9 years old, and one month) roughly has 3,500 days left in my house, give or take. Redeem the days and times for they are fleeting. Think for a moment of the impact all those Scripture studies, praise times, and prayer can accomplish in the days that remain with your kids. Send them out of your home like arrows from your quiver. Teach them the glorious deeds of God. Love them more than you fear their response or apathy. Serve them in ways they don't know they need to be served. Give your life to being their priest, and prophet, and shepherd.

Walk with other fathers: You are not alone in this work. Lock arms with other men and spur one another on to love and good works in these areas (Hebrews 10:24-25). Hold each other accountable. Ask each other questions and give advice. Pray for one another and each other's children.

Rest in God's grace: Fathers, we all fail in our responsibilities, and we must rest in the grace of God in Christ (Romans 4:16). Some of us have never led anything in our home, while others do it with a heavy hand or fear. No matter where we are in this, God's grace toward us abounds. If your kids are older and you have not led them well in these things, start now and rest on God's grace. We must encourage one another, not shame one another into obedience. These are heavy things, yet God's grace motivates us to be faithful (Romans 2:4). God does not forsake His people, He is with you.

Fear the Lord: The fear of the Lord is the beginning of wisdom (Proverbs 9:10). This is the instruction Solomon gave his son. And this is an instruction we should know to give to our children. The Lord delights in those who are humble and tremble at His Word (Isaiah 66:2). Do you tremble at what God's Word says?

Prepare the family: The worship in the home is always preparing for worship elsewhere. Keep in mind that we are preparing our families for corporate worship in our local churches each week as we set our hearts and minds on the Lord every day (not just Sundays). Our families should be ready and eager to be with other believers for corporate worship. This is the glorious church that God allows us to partake in. Family worship prepares for corporate worship. It also prepares them for the glorious worship we all will partake in when we worship at the feet of Christ when all of our knees are bowed and our tongues are confessing … that Jesus Christ is Lord!

These are important things. But remember, you are not alone in them. God gifted the church with pastors to care for the flock and minister God's Word to His people. This burden is shared, so enjoy it, and walk with other brothers together in it. God will be glorified, you will be sanctified, and your family will be blessed. The ancient paths are the right paths. By God's grace, walk in them!

APPENDIX A

A Neglected Grace by Jason Helopoulos

Gospel Family by Jonathan Williams

The Family Worship Book by Terry L. Johnson

D6 Family Ministries

A SAMPLE FAMILY WORSHIP STRUCTURE

READ and TEACH: Psalm 1

The Way of the Righteous and the Wicked

- Blessed is the man who walks not in the counsel of the wicked, nor stands in the way of sinners, nor sits in the seat of scoffers; but his delight is in the law of the Lord, and on his law he meditates day and night. He is like a tree planted by streams of water that yields its fruit in its season, and its leaf does not wither. In all that he does, he prospers. The wicked are not so, but are like chaff that the wind drives away. Therefore, the wicked will not stand in the judgment, nor sinners in the congregation of the righteous; for the Lord knows the way of the righteous, but the way of the wicked will perish.

Teach and Discuss:

- *What does the Law teach us about God? How does the text show this?*
- *Why is the Psalmist delighting in the Lord?*
- *What are the differences between one who delights in God and one who does not delight in God?*
- *What is one way you can apply this text to your daily life?*

111

PRAY: Psalm 1

- Psalm 1: Lord help us to delight in you and your Word. Father, we want to be like trees planted near streams of water. You are unique, the only One who fulfills the Law, and we praise You! (Adoration and Praise)

- Lord forgive us for when we do not delight in Your law or Your Word. We recognize our need for Jesus, but help us to grow in our affection for Him. (Confession)

- Thank you for allowing fruit to yield in our lives as a result of Your Word. We have seen the way of the righteous because You have graciously shown us the path. (Thanksgiving)

- Lord, we know the wicked are around us. Those who have not trusted in Your Word. Father, we lift up our neighbors and family members and ask that You would save them. Please give us opportunities to share Your glorious gospel. (Supplication)

MEMORIZE: Blessed is the man who walks not in the counsel of the wicked, nor stands in the way of sinners, nor sits in the seat of scoffers; but his delight is in the law of the Lord, and on his law he meditates day and night (Psalm 1:2).

PRAISE: *In Christ Alone* by Keith Getty & Stuart Townend.

APPENDIX B

GREAT RESOURCES FOR LEARNING MORE ABOUT FAMILY WORSHIP

A Neglected Grace: Family Worship in the Christian Home by Jason Helopoulos

Family Worship: In the Bible, in History, and in Your Home by Donald Whitney

Family Worship by Joel Beeke

Family Worship Guide by Joel Beeke

Family Shepherds: Calling and Equipping Men to Lead Their Homes by Voddie Baucham

Family Ministry Field Guide by Timothy Paul Jones

Family Worship: Biblical Basis, Historical Reality, Current Need by Kerry Ptacek

How Men Should Lead Their Families by Joel Beeke

Spurgeon's Catechism: With Scriptural Proofs by Charles Spurgeon

The Family Worship Book: A Resource Book for Family Devotions by Terry L. Johnson

The Duties of Parents: Parenting Your Children God's Way by J. C. Ryle

APPENDIX C

Key Components of *Metacognition*:

- Teachers must first recognize how they, themselves, learn new material and their own mental process of learning.[1]

- A helpful question for a teacher to ask; "Have you paused in your lesson preparation to consider how you went about learning the concepts you are preparing to teach?"[2]

- Tactics inside of the metacognition: strengthen memory, identifying most important points of passages, writing down important reflections, and developing a "coding" system for when passages have several different ideas; all ultimately meant to help the learner connect the information in their own minds.[3]

Key Components of *Reflection*:

- The Teacher considers his/her own evaluation of his/her effectiveness as a teacher.

- Best practices: evaluating and making adjustments as actions from the learners are considered, discussing best practices with other teachers, and thinking through the discipline of teaching and things to consider the next time one teaches.[4]

Active Learning Techniques:

- Reflection on a particular point of the text

- Interaction with Scripture (reading through passage several times)

- Writing exercises to enhance reflection and assessment (if able)

The 5Cs: A Simple Lesson Outline for Fathers to Give Instruction

- *Chunk: ten-minute intervals*
- *Challenge: a targeted question*
- *Chew: allotted amount of time for learner to consider*
- *Chat: learner is provided opportunity to express understanding*
- *Check: teacher gives a final targeted question for understanding and allows students to respond (summary of main point).*

Endnotes ─────────────────────────────────────

[1] Coley, *Teaching for Change*, 50-51.

[2] Ibid., 51.

[3] Ibid., 54-55.

[4] Ibid., 56-58.

The **D6** Family App

Available in App Stores

Updated weekly, this app delivers
resources designed to equip you
for generational discipleship.

D6 Resources Included:

- Family Fun Questions
- SPLINK
- Parent Pages
- Family Fun Nights
- Foundational Talks
- The D6 Podcast
- Blog

AND MORE!

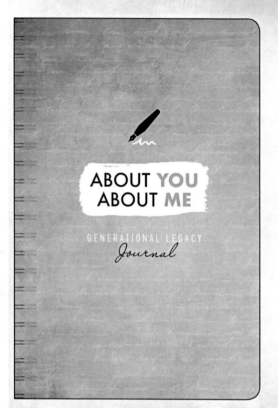